Palgrave Studies in Translating and Interpreting

Series Editor
Margaret Rogers
Department of Languages and Translation
University of Surrey
Guildford, United Kingdom

This series examines the crucial role which translation and interpreting in their myriad forms play at all levels of communication in today's world, from the local to the global. Whilst this role is being increasingly recognised in some quarters (for example, through European Union legislation), in others it remains controversial for economic, political and social reasons. The rapidly changing landscape of translation and interpreting practice is accompanied by equally challenging developments in their academic study, often in an interdisciplinary framework and increasingly reflecting commonalities between what were once considered to be separate disciplines. The books in this series address specific issues in both translation and interpreting with the aim not only of charting and but also of shaping the discipline with respect to contemporary practice and research.

More information about this series at
http://www.springer.com/series/14574

Renée Desjardins

Translation and Social Media

In Theory, in Training and in Professional Practice

Renée Desjardins
School of Translation
University of Saint-Boniface
Winnipeg, Canada

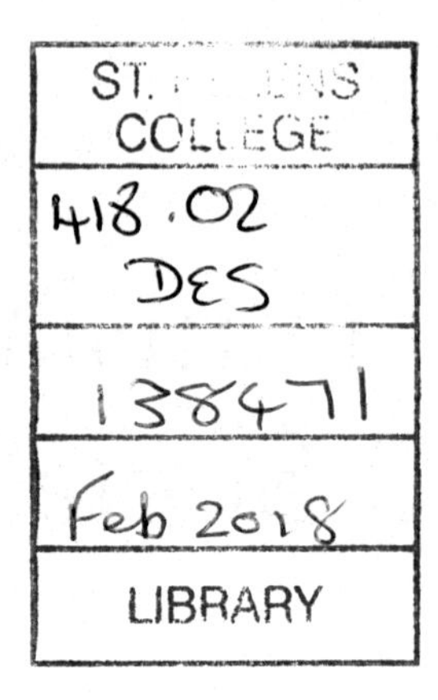

Palgrave Studies in Translating and Interpreting
ISBN 978-1-137-52254-2 ISBN 978-1-137-52255-9 (eBook)
DOI 10.1057/978-1-137-52255-9

Library of Congress Control Number: 2016952435

Printed on acid-free paper

This Palgrave Pivot imprint is published by Springer Nature
The registered company is Macmillan Publishers Ltd.
The registered company address is: The Campus, 4 Crinan Street, London, N1 9XW, United Kingdom

For my brother Eric; for my parents; for Chris; for my friends (many thanks to MP, HMc, HG and TVB, in particular); for my mentors; and especially for my students, who have inspired every part of this book: thank you so much for your patience, your generosity and your unwavering support. As well, a debt of gratitude goes to all those who helped me get from there to here, and also to the Reeds, who allowed me to use their ranch as my writing retreat.

Acknowledgements

My sincere thanks to the Palgrave Macmillan team, specifically Margaret Rogers for her insight and suggestions.

Contents

List of Abbreviations

CAT	Computer-assisted translation
ICT	Information and communication technologies
MT	Machine translation (usually automatic machine translation)
OSM	Online social media
SEO	Search engine optimization
SMM	Social media management and monitoring
ST	Source text
TM	Translation memory
TS	Translation studies
TT	Target text
UGC	User-generated content
UGT	User-generated translation

List of Figures

CHAPTER 1

Introduction

Abstract Translation and online social media (OSM): what do these areas have in common? Why is it now relevant to analyse the relationship between these two areas of study? How is studying translation in the context of OSM any different from scholarship already produced in the areas of crowdsourced translation or online collaborative translation? Or localization? This introductory chapter presents arguments supporting greater inquiry into the connections between translation and social media. Citing work from Littau (*Translation Studies*, 4(3): 261–281, 2011; *Translation Studies* 9(1): 82–96, 2015) and Munday (*Introducing translation studies.* 4th edition, 2016), among others, on the topics of new materialities and new media, the author argues that translation and OSM afford a rich and complex area of study. This chapter maps the increase in popularity of social media and its significance today to underscore why this topic is of particular relevance in contemporary translation studies. The chapter also provides a chapter-by-chapter overview of the book's content.

Keywords Translation · Social media · Crowdsourced translation · Collaborative translation · Localization

In a recent and extremely thought-provoking article, Littau (2015) asserts that the role that media plays in shaping our thoughts and our words, and thus human communication more generally, has been relatively ignored in scholarship produced within the humanities. She argues that for far too

R. Desjardins, *Translation and Social Media*, Palgrave Studies in Translating and Interpreting, DOI 10.1057/978-1-137-52255-9_1

long, language, meaning and interpretation have been the central foci in the humanities, and especially in translation studies (TS), to the detriment of other 'materialities' – material technologies and techniques – that also inherently shape and play a role in human communication. Her line of thought runs parallel to some of Pym's (2011a, online) observations in which he states:

> Technology [...] extends the ways we interact with our world: our arms, our sight, our capacity to hear, touch, to move over distances. [...] The technologies of transport and communication radically stretch the cross-cultural situations in which speech acts are carried out, ultimately altering the configuration of cultures, never more so than in a globalizing age.

Indeed, if we think about how translation occurs today in professional settings, who can imagine working without a computer? Or word-processing software? Or online reference materials? And yet, it is only in more recent years that researchers in TS have been considering the ways in which technology impacts *how* translators translate. In fact, in Canada, some are debating whether or not translators are even now necessary in some scenarios, given the increased reliability of automatic machine translation (MT) and of computer-assisted translation (CAT) technologies (cf. Delisle 2016; 'Online translator helps federal workers "do their job", say defenders' 2016). Eye-tracking and key-tracking technologies, for instance, have made it possible to see how translators interact with screens and keyboards when carrying out their translations (Koglin 2015; Law 2015) – a topic that was at the forefront of the fifth International Association of Translation and Intercultural Studies conference, *Innovation paths in translation and intercultural studies*, held in Belo Horizonte, Brazil, in July 2015. Generally, this research has shown very tangibly that technology does indeed impact the translation process: that translators' decisions and actions while interacting with computers are not necessarily those they would have taken had they been working with only a piece of paper and pencil. Studies of the richly complex topic of human–machine interaction in the context of translation processes can show us how technology and media intersect not only with what we can communicate, but *how* we communicate. As Littau asserts: 'Media [technology and by extension associated "media cultures"] are not merely instruments with which writers or translators produce meanings; rather, they *set the framework within which something like meaning becomes possible at all*' (2015, p. 2, emphasis in original).

Studying online phenomena is a challenging endeavour as it essentially constitutes trying to steady a moving target: technology, today, adapts and evolves far more quickly than ever before. By the time this book has been published, it is likely that new social platforms will have already gained more popularity and that new devices will have hit the market, perhaps making some of the examples and discussion points presented here already obsolete. Some online social media (OSM) platforms have even undergone design overhauls in the few months it took to write the manuscript (cf. 'A New Look for Instagram' 2016). Though studying translation in current media culture – a media culture that is largely centred around OSM, incidentally – presents many challenges, including the rapid rate at which some observations can become obsolete, it is the only way to create a base for future research to keep apace with technological advancement.

Translation and OSM: what do these areas have in common? Why is it now relevant to analyse the relationship between these two areas of study and practice? How is studying translation in the context of OSM any different from scholarship already produced in the areas of crowdsourced translation or online collaborative translation? Or localization?

We may partially answer the question *Why is the study of the relationships between translation and OSM relevant for today's translators?* by stating that OSM is now a predominant 'materiality' or 'mediality' (to use Littau's terminology) that underpins a significant percentage of our daily interactions, from writing, to reading, to translating, to even producing culture more broadly. Munday (2016, p. 317) even concludes his most recent edition of *Introducing Translation Studies* by stating the advance of new technologies, and more specifically social media, is resulting in the emergence of new forms of interaction 'where translation is playing an important role'. However, Munday's (*ibid.*) chapter on New Media doesn't tackle social media and translation head-on, suggesting that this area of study is relatively under-researched.

In 2006, *Time*'s person of the year was 'You' (Grossman 2006). The decision was based on the argument that Web 2.0 now afforded everyone with an Internet connection and basic OSM skills the option of creating *Facebook* profiles detailing the minutiae of their lives; of blogging on everything from political campaigns to last night's dinner; and of collaborating with their fellow global citizens in absolutely unprecedented ways. A study by UM Social Media Tracker Wave 5 (2010) found that 'almost 75 % of the active Internet universe has used online social networking sites, and almost half of them have joined an online brand community' (Singh et al. 2012, p. 684).[1] According to eMarketer, 'a research source for marketing in a digital world', in 2014, 68.6 % of Internet users in the United States used social networks, while in Canada, the figure was 68 % ('Canada Neck and Neck…', 2014). In 2018, eMarketer ('Social Network Audience…', 2015) forecasts that 70.6 % of Canadian Internet users will access social networks monthly, which represents roughly 59.9 % of the Canadian population, an anticipated rise of 2.6 %. These data show that interaction with OSM is significant on an international scale, and that in some countries, like Canada, rates of interaction are still rising. Thus, from *Time* declaring 'You' to be central in the social landscape, to increasing rates of OSM activity, OSM is impacting, rather significantly, some aspects of human communication. It follows then that OSM must also be impacting translation, from how translators translate, to *what type of content* translators are translating, to the very languages that are being translated on these social applications and platforms. These areas constitute the focal points of this book and will be considered under the umbrella of three overarching themes: theory, training and professional practice.

Although we are relatively far from initial concerns about primacy to source texts and word-level equivalence – dominant trends in the early 'turns' of TS (Snell-Hornby 2009), which date back to when translation was studied within the paradigm of comparative literature (Snell-Hornby 2006) – the questions now being raised by the relationships between translation and OSM fall squarely in line with more recent advancements in contemporary TS inquiry, such as studying 'the effects of technology and globalization' (Snell-Hornby 2012, p. 370) and studying 'new forms of interaction' (Munday 2016, p. 317). Connections between translation and social media can also be made in light of other 'turns'. The 'sociological turn' in TS scholarship, for instance, has given increasing attention 'to the agency of translators and interpreters, as well as to the social factors that permeate acts of translation interpreting' (Angelelli 2014). The 'sociological turn' (*ibid.*) has also seen the rise of more studies focusing on the role translation can and does play in resistance and activist movements (Tymoczko 2010; Baker 2015) and in affording or negating access to knowledge and cultural capital (Buzelin 2005; Brisset 2010). OSM constitute one of the contexts in which significant activist and social movements gain momentum; they are also one of the main sources people now consult to consume and circulate content, be it news content, social content, art content, literary content, visual content and so on. In fact, research merging both sociological approaches and activism in social media contexts has already started to take shape, though this area still constitutes a relatively small niche in TS. Colòn Rodriguez (2013), for instance, has studied activist translation in Canada, specifically with regard to the 'Translating the printemps érable' movement.[2] In the case of 'Translating the printremps érable' activist 'translators' challenged incorrect press reports and managed to reach a more wide-ranging audience in Canada and beyond. In another era, it would have been perhaps unimaginable that a group of citizens, perhaps without formal journalism training or translation training, would have been able to mobilize and (re)translate news articles that didn't adequately represent a series of events. Moreover, if we apply Littau's (2015) thinking here, we see that OSM is the specific 'tool' (mediality) that has given these Web 2.0 'citizen-translators' the platform and means to carry out their work. It follows then that better understanding of OSM can give TS researchers more insight into these types of online social movements and activist movements.

Further, while it can be said that investigation into the relationships between technology and translation is nothing new and in fact predates the constitution of the field itself (Holmes 1972, 1988/2004), Littau's (2011, 2015) and Pym's (2011a) observations and reflections seem to indicate a new direction in TS, one that Cronin (2013) has also chosen to explore in his work connecting translation and the 'digital age'. While other scholars have explored *translation technologies* (i.e. MT and CAT tools) (e.g. Sin-Wai 2015) and *localization* (here, to be understood in a limited and strict sense, i.e. the translation of strings of text intended for software, application or website localization) (e.g. Jiménez-Crespo 2013), few have addressed how the 'digital age' might be creating paradigmatic shifts within TS. The intent of this book, then, is not to explore translation as an interlinguistic operation occurring simply in a different medium (i.e. interlinguistic translation from paper to hypertext, to play on Vandendorpe's *From Papyrus to Hypertext* [2009]), or how computer-assisted tools can facilitate or hinder the process, but rather how OSM is helping to reconfigure important aspects of the profession and the field: from impacting the texts and discourses that are being translated, to introducing new iconographic languages (e.g. *Emoji*; see Chap. 3), and to shifting the very identities of translators themselves. While studies in localization address how to adapt the translation process to account for specific software constraints and cultural requirements so that a product's reception might be favourable in a given target market, the context in which localization occurs is not the same as, say, a translator having to translate a *tweet* on *Twitter* using appropriate hashtags. There are certainly similarities that can be drawn between localization and translation occurring on OSM. And localization has undoubtedly paved the way for some of the strategies seen and used in social media content translation. However, the *context* and the *reasons* for translation on social media are not always commercially motivated (i.e. who commissions the translation matters), and when they are, the approach taken is somewhat different. Game localization, for instance, is meant to ensure that video games can be played by video game enthusiasts regardless of geographic locale. Software localization is meant to ensure software suites and programmes can be used (read: bought) by a greater number of computer users. And while translating a company's social media content (be it *tweets* or *status updates* that promote a given product) can certainly have a commercial objective, this is not systematically the case. OSM, in this sense, affords a sort of 'democratic' translation environment: anyone who is bilingual and relatively fluent in 'OSM speak' can translate content and make it available to new audiences, sometimes in support of certain ideological or political agendas, or sometimes only to share content that would appeal to a given fan-base, as is the case with fansubbing or fandubbing sites (O'Hagan 2008, 2009). Translation on OSM doesn't necessarily mean that an individual has accreditation or diplomas, nor does it even suggest that an individual has expert proficiency in any given language pair. This has significant ramifications for the future of translation: what are the implications of this reality for translator training, accreditation and remuneration? How can professional translators 'stand out' and justify their fee when 'cost-free' collaborative and crowdsourced translation continues to increase in popularity? How can we impart new translation skills in line with the 'digital age' such that translator trainees will be as competitive as their peers graduating from computer programming or creative communications programmes? CAT and MT training in this context is unfortunately insufficient, a topic that will be covered in Chap. 4 in greater detail.

In 1993, Lefevere wrote that TS 'suffered' from insularity, reinventing the wheel, and often forgetting its own history. More than 20 years later, some might argue this is still the case. This book certainly owes a debt to previous TS researchers who have already contributed to this burgeoning area. The book will, however, introduce an unprecedented framework for thinking critically about the relationships between translation and OSM in three key areas (theory, training and practice) and will use real-world examples to further elucidate. The book attempts to avoid insularity by drawing insight from other disciplines, chiefly media and communication studies (within which social media studies tend to be subsumed), web design, computer science, cultural studies and others. Inasmuch as history is relevant to the topics discussed, attempts will be made to draw from earlier work in TS to compare and contrast contemporary thinking on translation and translation practice. Though most of the examples are drawn from the author's experience as a Canadian researcher and translator, this is not to say the book's content is specific to Canada alone; social media, after all, largely escape the confines of nation-states. And a final caveat: a number of references from beyond scholarly publications are included in support of some ideas and arguments. Given the contemporary and evolving nature of the book's topic, recourse to these types of references seemed justified. In essence, much like OSM, this book is intended to engage its readership in an ongoing conversation.

The second chapter provides an overview of OSM, including important definitions and the historical development of social media. Although popular belief suggests that social media is new, this is not the case. The journalist Tom Standage (2013), for instance, aptly illustrates how the concept of 'social media' is not completely revolutionary, nor is it as radical as we may think. That said, *OSM* is a new iteration of 'social media' and will constitute the focal type of social media addressed within these pages. In addition, Chap. 2 will outline the main differences between Web 1.0 and Web 2.0. Although other scholars (e.g. Folaron 2010a) have mapped the Web's history in TS, this chapter will seek to add a few additional insights to the existing literature. The intent is not, as Lefevere (1993) indicates, to ignore or repeat work that has already been done, but rather to offer readers of this book a 'one-stop' reference that overviews both web and social media history in relation to translation, particularly for those readers that may not have much web expertise or social media knowledge. Chapter 2, moreover, lists six key areas in which research on translation and social media has begun, and identifies areas that may warrant further investigation and empirical contributions, including those that comprise the book's other chapters (Chaps. 3, 4 and 5).

Chapter 3 considers how OSM can impact translation theories and concepts in TS. It starts with an analysis of some of the changes in human communicational behaviour that have been brought on by OSM.

This chapter also considers how language is changing or, rather, adapting to the social media landscape, which includes the use of hashtags and *Emoji*. When we consider that 'Emoji'– a 'language' made up of colourful symbols which currently boasts an adoption rate worthy of further investigation (Bangor University 2015) – now constitutes the *lingua franca* on social platforms such as *Instagram*, are interlinguistic definitions of translation sufficient to explain and study this type of online phenomena? These changes, it is argued, make Jakobson's (1959/2004) *intersemiotic* definition of translation particularly prescient, and set the stage for increased discussion of multimodality and different semiotic systems within TS. Then, drawing on critical theory in social media studies (Fuchs 2014, 2015), this chapter re-explores the concepts of power, knowledge, labour and time in TS, but here, more specifically in the context of the new 'social media economy' (the 'like' economy). For instance, when power is no longer measured by economic wealth alone, but rather in the form of *Facebook* '*likes*' and *Twitter* '*retweets*' (a form of symbolic remuneration, or what McDonough Dolmaya [2011] refers to as 'non-monetary incentives'), what could this mean for translation and for translators? Are the 'new translators' looking to be paid by the word or by the '*like*'? Especially when '*likes*' can translate (pun intended) into corporate sponsorships or crowd validation? Consideration will be given to the concept of 'augmentation' (Davenport and Kirby 2015) and its relevance in this debate.

The fourth chapter examines how current translator training and education is not addressing key competencies needed for the 'digital age', with specific focus given to translation programmes within Canadian universities as an example. With a narrow focus on language, interlinguistic translation, specific media competencies and 'teaching for accreditation exams', Canadian translation programmes are not wholly addressing contemporary market realities or prospective competition from other industry sectors. At a time when the Canadian Translation Bureau is cutting jobs and rolling out a new automation platform, the arguments for revamping training are imperative. While no translation programme can address every aspect of professional translation, this chapter argues in favour of integrating OSM literacy and competency within the translation curriculum. Although this seems ambitious, some strategies are proposed throughout the chapter that might be helpful to those teaching undergraduate and graduate translation courses or for those trying to fine-tune their own skills. These strategies might also provide inspiration for other curriculum developments. The underlying argument is that if translator trainees are not taught OSM competencies, they will not be able to compete with bilinguals with more 'attractive' profiles, particularly 'elite bilinguals' with computer programing, web design or communications backgrounds. While localization courses can offer some relevant technical expertise, OSM translation and software localization do not necessarily follow the same protocols, rules and processes. Some might suggest that teaching to the market falls into a professionalization and corporatization of university education that is not necessarily appropriate or in line with the core values of post-secondary education (Giroux 2007). This is the paradox of teaching translation in a university setting: most translation students, ultimately, want a job, and preferably a job in translation. While there is much to be gained in a literary translation course, for instance, the reality is that paid work in this sector is fraught with challenges and remarkably difficult to find, especially for a young graduate 'fresh' out of the classroom. The idea then is not to replace what is generally assumed to be more 'creative' or 'theoretically focused' coursework, but rather to strike a balance between critical thinking, critical training and what is necessary for navigating an increasingly complex and technical marketplace. This chapter directly addresses Brisset's (2010) call for 'new teaching' that addresses new forms of interlinguistic and intercultural mediation, brought forward by new technologies and new global realities; in other words, *social skills* are as important as *technical skills*. And if the new 'social' is OSM, then it follows that OSM should be part of this 'new teaching'.

Chapter 5 addresses the relationships between OSM and the professional translation market, and more specifically, how professional translators are leveraging OSM in creative, and sometimes surprisingly lucrative and beneficial, ways. By defining translation as a 'social activity' (O'Hagan 2011) and building on social systems theories applied in TS (Tyulenev 2011, 2014) as well as network theories applied in TS (Folaron 2010b), this chapter considers the ways in which translators self-describe their work and role on various OSM platforms, with emphasis given to activity on *LinkedIn* (an OSM platform that caters specifically to online professional networking). Here, the link with the past is clear: there was a time when translators were considered 'invisible', forced to 'live' under the author's name or, worse, never to be 'seen' at all – a topic that is most often associated with Venuti's well-known publication *The Translator's Invisibility* (1995, 2008). Contemporary literary texts may now make more frequent acknowledgement of translators and their work – which is generally positive – yet, in many other instances, particularly in the case of administrative translation, translators and their work continue to be unacknowledged. This chapter will argue, however, that OSM affords translators a new visibility, regardless of the type of translation they do professionally. With online professional networking sites, complete with pictures and real-time updates, translators can now have a digital presence and a digital voice. This new digital 'visibility' is surely good, is it not? After all, for so long, research in TS has sought to 'unveil' the very people – the translators – who have helped disseminate knowledge (cf. Delisle 1999, 2002), such that they be seen and recognized for their contributions. But, could there be a downside to this new digital 'visibility'? Does translating *tweets, statuses* and other forms of user-generated content paradoxically contribute to the translator's invisibility?

Earlier drafts of the book included specific chapters that focused on individual OSM platforms (e.g. Chap. 2 *Facebook*; Chap. 3 *Twitter*; etc.). However, given the shifting nature of these platforms and the demographics associated with them, this breakdown seemed unnecessarily artificial and subject to making the content quickly obsolete. Instead, by posing broader questions and using platform-specific examples to illustrate some of the ideas and hypotheses, the belief is that this book will have a longer lifespan. After all, who now talks about ICQ and AOL? And some millennial readers may not even remember an era before *Facebook*...

While no publication can purport to speak to all potential audiences, this book is intended for a wide array of readers, be it undergraduate students enrolled in a translation programme, graduate students in TS, media studies and/or other related fields, professional translators, translator trainers and educators. The content is also meant to 'bridge' the gap between theorization and professional practice, as these are often (unfortunately) considered separately (Munday 2012, p. 25). The hope is that professional translators will see the importance of theory in considering how new technologies (or 'materialities' to use Littau's terminology) are radically changing the profession. In turn, researchers cannot ignore what is happening in the industry. Perhaps what Lefevere failed to address in 1993 was not so much the repetitive or insular content produced in TS, but rather the lack of a symbiotic and mutually beneficial discourse that is insightful not only for two major audiences (theorists and practitioners), but also for two often neglected audiences as well: workshop trainers and undergraduate students. This book also aims to speak to millennial translators (who are ostensibly the 'new' generation), certainly, but to other generations of translators as well. It is also inspired by many voices and conversations held with former students, translator colleagues and renowned translation scholars alike.

If you would like to contribute to the conversation beyond these pages, the author regularly monitors conversations using #SocialMedia and #Translation.

Notes

1. Please also see Social Media Tracker's Wave 4 report (2009).
2. The Quebecois 'printemps érable' (Maple Spring) movement was formed in response to proposed post-secondary tuition hikes and changes to post-secondary bursary and funding programmes in the spring of 2012 (Houpt 2012). Initially, the Anglophone Canadian media did not cover the events, and when they finally did, the facts seemed to be skewed or 'mis-translated' according to 'printemps érable' group members. Thus, these members sought to provide 'better' and 'more adequate' translations of the original French-language press articles covering the events related to the 'printemps érable'. They describe their work as follows: 'Translating the printemps érable is a volunteer collective initiated in an attempt to balance the English media's extremely poor coverage of the student conflict in Québec by translating media that has been published in French into English' ('Translating the printemps érable' 2012).

CHAPTER 2

Online Social Media (OSM) and Translation

Abstract Chapter 2 provides an overview of the evolution of online social media (OSM), including important definitions and an overview of historical developments. This constitutes essential reading for translation students, professionals and translation studies (TS) researchers who may not be familiar with the broader history of the Web and OSM. Following a brief overview of areas in TS that intersect with OSM, Chap. 2 further details six key areas in which research on translation and social media has begun (e.g. crowdsourcing, fan translation and online activism) and identifies potential research avenues, some of which constitute the focal points of the book's following chapters.

Keywords Online social media · Web · TS · Translation · Social media · Crowdsourcing · Fan translation · Activism

2.1 Online Social Media: An Overview

Social media. Fifteen years ago, this term was far from the mainstream collective consciousness. The umbrella term 'media' tends to now connote 'traditional' media, that is the press (or print journalism in general), television, advertising and film. Although traditional media is inherently 'social', impacting social relations and society in various ways, this form of 'sociality' (i.e. how individuals tend to associate in groups) differs vastly from today's social media, which tend to be synonymous with *online* social media (OSM)

R. Desjardins, *Translation and Social Media*, Palgrave Studies in Translating and Interpreting, DOI 10.1057/978-1-137-52255-9_2

(as we shall see, the distinction matters). Traditional media of the past generally functioned according to a top-down model, in which only specific institutions and individuals (usually a more powerful elite) generated and shared content. For instance, although readers could write comments to their local newspapers, prior to the mainstream use of the Web, this constituted a vested form of engagement – and one that rarely resulted in instant communication or validation. Therefore, the argument could be made that fewer individuals felt enough incentive to engage directly with 'traditional' media institutions. In contrast, today's social media indicate a significant shift: lines are blurred between who is producing content and who is responding to it. As the *Frontline* documentary from the US Public Broadcasting Service *Generation Like* (2014) asserts, users and producers of social media content engage in a symbiotic exchange of information, in an endless communicative loop. Gone are the days when only the few could share information or disseminate knowledge; today, anyone with access to the Web and an electronic device, be it a mobile phone, tablet or computer (laptop or desktop), can contribute to 'the conversation'. In this sense, one could make the argument that today's social media is significantly more democratic and social than previous forms of traditional media. But is this truly the case? And is social media really as new and novel as we think it is?

It is important to examine the evolution of social media and to contextualize what it is we mean when we say *social* media. Many make the easy mistake of thinking social media is new and revolutionary; however, this is not the case: 'Social media is not new. Media has been leveraged for sociable purposes since the caveman's walls. [. . .] For decades, we've watched the development of new genres of social media' (boyd 2009, online). Likewise, in a remarkably illuminating book – *Writing on the Wall: Social Media – The first Two Thousand Years* – Tom Standage, digital editor at *The Economist*, explains that there is nothing innately novel about social media, even though the tendency is to think otherwise. Rather, what has changed, significantly, is the medium on which and the speed at which communication now occurs. Indeed, Standage makes the case that humans have an inherent need for sharing, and because of this need, they have *always* found ways of sharing. Thus, social media are as old as the human need to communicate; he states:

> Humans are, in short, built to form networks with others and to exchange information with them. [. . .] The compelling nature of social media, then,

> can be traced back in part to the evolution of the social brain [. . .] [and] in part to the exchange of gossip following the emergence of human language, around one hundred thousand years ago; and in part to the origins of writing, around five thousand years ago. These are the [. . .] ancient foundations on which the social sharing of media, whether using papyrus scrolls in Roman times or the Internet today, has rested over the past two millennia. (2013, p. 8)

Further, even though traditional media may seem less 'social' than contemporary understandings of social media (for instance, the aforementioned newspaper reader example), this is perhaps misleading. If, as Fuchs (2014) explains, being social is defined as being part of society, then any type of social engagement, however passive, could be viewed as 'social'. In other words, inasmuch as someone writes in their diary, they are contributing to the social world: the ideas and emotions being recorded reflect a relationship with the social world and what is happening in society at that given time. Watching television, even though seemingly passive, can be social in that the television content likely represents various aspects of society at that moment in history, such as social norms, for instance. Thus, the idea that social media today are *more* social than other forms of traditional media, such as books or magazines, can be relativized. What creates the illusion of increased sociality in today's OSM is the higher degree of information sharing, collaboration and community building they afford (Standage 2013), as well as the sheer speed at which information can be shared, disseminated and processed.

Translation, in a sense, shares a similar history. Globalization has undoubtedly increased contact between different cultures and different languages; therefore, it might be tempting to view translation as a relatively recent phenomenon. However, here, Cronin (2013) does for translation what Standage has done for social media. In *Translation and the Digital Age*, Cronin shows that translation has been a key vector in what he calls the '3T paradigm' (technology, trade and translation) throughout much of human history. Inasmuch as humans have had a need for sharing and forming networks, they have also had to trade to ensure survival. This in turn meant the development of new technology and the need to overcome potential deterrents to trade, of which the inability to communicate in an unknown language is but one example. Cue the need, then, for translation.

Through Standage's and Cronin's work, we see then that social media and translation have evolved somewhat similarly and in a parallel fashion:

ever-present since the early days of human interaction, but shifting in form and increasing in speed and inefficiency over the centuries. As Standage (2013) explains, whereas orators once acted as the 'social media' of the Roman Empire, today, people flock to social media platforms such as *Facebook* and *Twitter* to obtain the latest news, gossip or family update. And while translation and interpretation were once carried out using rudimentary tools, today, translation can be done significantly faster in some cases through the use of various computer-assisted translation programs or even automatic machine translation, of which *Google Translate* is but one example. In fact, today's social media and translation technology are so intertwined that it is now possible to have OSM content translated automatically in real time.

That said, although 'social media' can refer to virtually any form of media used to foster and expand human networks, and although it is a 'complex term with multi-layered meanings' (Fuchs 2014, p. 6), here, attention will, as stated, be drawn specifically to OSM. Though other definitions exist, including more recent ones,[1] the definition proposed by Kaplan and Haenlein (2010) is at once broad enough to account for most forms of OSM discussed in these pages, but not so broad as to encompass all the various forms of social media that Standage (2013) addresses (i.e. 'traditional' or 'analog' social media, meaning media that does not require a digital signal or use of a digital device). Kaplan and Haenlein define OSM as user-generated content (UGC) that is created, exchanged and curated on Web 2.0 platforms and applications. What is particularly relevant in their definition is the focus on the 'user', rather than strictly on the technology, the latter usually being the focal point in other definitions. For instance, Fuchs (2014) and boyd and Ellison's (2008) definitions state that the term OSM refers to the online *media, software, web-based services and applications* that allow users to share, to collaborate, to gather and to communicate. While it is certainly the case that OSM should be understood as encompassing *both* UGC and the media/technologies that enable the dissemination of UGC, this can sometimes pose challenges when a distinction between the two is necessary. From a translation perspective, a definition of OSM that focuses on UGC and the users themselves aligns more directly with current theoretical trends that seek to shed light on power relations, networks and agency. A definition of OSM that too narrowly focuses on the media/technology, one could argue, tends to intersect more directly with localization: i.e. translation of the applications or sites themselves, as opposed to the translation of UGC occurring or being disseminated *on* the applications or sites – the nuance is slight, but significant. Because web localization is a topic that has been discussed in greater detail and at greater length by other translation studies (TS) scholars, for instance, Esselink (2000, 2003), Schäler (2010), Pym (2011b), Jiménez-Crespo (2013), and Dunne (2015), the perspective taken here is slightly different. Localization usually coincides with translation for a market purpose (i.e. commercial purpose), and Schäler's and Dunne's definitions, in particular, underscore this, as does Cronin (2003, p. 63) when he states: 'With its emphasis on target-oriented translation, wholly consonant with the more popular versions of functional and polysystem theories of translation, "localization" appears to be the *corporate linguistic response* to the ecological injunction think global and act local' (emphasis added). Moreover, much of the research on localization tends to focus on different workflow models (i.e. the localization process) and does not necessarily invoke philosophical or theoretical insight to problematize these. Further, the translation of social media content *by individual users* might, unlike corporate localized content, be intentionally or inadvertently guided by a source-oriented approach either because these users want to underscore the foreign nature of their content or because they may 'simply' lack formal translation training or maybe even because they turned to embedded automatic machine translation (e.g. *Bing* translation on *Facebook*). This is why, here, localization and OSM translation (in general terms) are not viewed as synonymous. While they share commonalities, such as being Web-based phenomena and favourable to cross-cultural communication, there are significant differences, the most notable being that of *who* is translating and why. In OSM translation, translation is not reserved to a specialized workforce (i.e. professional translators or localizers); *everyone* can, ostensibly, translate. The rules of localization do not necessarily apply, therefore, in the translation of UGC. This is why Kaplan and Haenlein's definition of OSM is particularly engaging: there is less of a focus on market-driven activity, workflow processes and technology and more emphasis given to how users communicate among and for themselves, which includes phenomena in which users are the translators/localizers of their own content. This user-centred definition of OSM, moreover, resonates with the 2006 *Times'* article (Grossman 2006) that placed the individual (i.e. 'you the user') at the centre of a 'massive social experiment'.

However, this brief definition of OSM may not be helpful to those who are unfamiliar with web jargon and the Web's history, for instance, the distinctions to be made between Web 1.0 and 2.0, the evolution of OSM and the differences in content produced on different OSM platforms. The history of OSM is directly connected to the history of the Internet and, more specifically, the Web, as Standage aptly explains in a chapter dedicated to the rise of *Facebook*. In the late 1960s and early 1970s, researchers in California were seeking to link computers to reduce the number of computer terminals in offices. A subsidiary goal was to facilitate collaboration between different institutions, and, by extension, different researchers in different geographical locations. This system, which would eventually be known as ARPANET, was the first iteration of what we now know today as the Internet. In 1975, the ARPANET system became fully functional and eventually it linked different computer networks, as opposed to individual terminals, a process known as 'internetting'. In the 1980s, ARPANET started to be known as the Internet. From there, users of the network were able to send personal messages (early iterations of email) that led to the creation of mailing lists and newsgroups. Communication could now occur in unprecedented ways.

In the late 1980s and 1990s, home and personal computers became increasingly popular and more and more people were willing to invest in the necessary hardware and software to experience this new connectivity. Unfortunately, Internet uptake was not entirely user-friendly: connections depended on the availability of phone lines and various software suites. Online information was disjointed, largely passive (i.e. read-only), and still only accessible to an economic and technical elite. Although some early personal computers sold for 'only' 400–600 US dollars (Ahl 1984), this did not factor in other associated costs such as landlines, modems and other hardware.

In 1993, in a step towards a more accessible, and according to some, democratic Internet, Tim Berners-Lee, a British scientist, wrote the programme known as the World Wide Web (Standage 2013). This led to the creation of the first Web 'browsers', which included Mosaic (the first browser to make the Web accessible to the general public), followed by Netscape Navigator. This first 'phase' of the Web, in which most content was read-only and devoid of significant multimedia content (including video, sound, animations or a combination of these), is predominantly referred to as *Web 1.0*. During this time, the translation of web content was usually conducted offline with word processing software, only to be uploaded at a later juncture, either by a webmaster or web programmer. This marked the start towards more sophisticated approaches to localization and multimedia translation.

By the year 2000, roughly 250 million people were 'connected' (*ibid.*). Various organizations, from universities to brick-and-mortar stores, quickly realized the Web's potential for creating an online presence. Though these web pages and sites were, in essence, created by 'users', they did not facilitate two-way communication *between* users. In other words, when Web users consulted a given page, they could not interact with the content, say, by leaving a review or a comment, or uploading a picture or video. Moreover, with Web 1.0, those developing web-based technology followed a model that went from product development, to testing, to being available to consumers; there was no user interaction at the phase of product development. But this would eventually change.

Online social networking, that is the process of creating social networks via web pages and sites, started to take shape in 1997 with the creation of *Six Degrees* (boyd and Ellison 2008). Thanks to this site, users could see how they were connected to other users, based on 'degrees' of separation. The site ultimately shut down in 2000, but it generated significant interest in the Web's potential for creating and sustaining social networks between users and paved the way for early social networking sites (SNSs) including *Friendster*, which launched in 2002, and *MySpace*, which launched in late 2003 (*ibid.*). It was around this time that the term 'Web 2.0' started to gain currency. Web 2.0 marked a shift from a predominantly read-only interface to an interactive, read–write interface. As boyd (2009, online) explains:

> For the technology crowd, Web 2.0 was about a shift in development and deployment. Rather than producing a product, testing it, and shipping it to be consumed by an audience that was disconnected from the developer, Web 2.0 was about the perpetual beta. [. . .] for technologists, Web 2.0 was about constantly iterating the technology as people interacted with it and learning from what they were doing. To make this happen, we saw the rise of technologies that supported real-time interactions, user-generated content, remixing and mashups, APIs [Application Program Interface] and open-source software that allowed mass collaboration in the development cycle. [. . .] *This was a critical disruption in the way in which technology was historically produced.* [emphasis added]

Thus, Web 2.0 afforded users and developers the option not only of uploading and disseminating content, but also of interacting with other users/developers in unprecedented ways. Web 2.0 was about getting users to connect in new ways. *MySpace*, for instance, eventually became the most popular of the SNSs of the time, reaching a hundred million users in 2006 and becoming the fifth most popular site in the United States (Standage 2013). *MySpace* gave users the option of creating custom profiles (a precursor to the *Facebook* profile), uploading some types of media content (sound clips and photo avatars, for instance) and generating friend lists. If any site at the time embodied the early spirit of Web 2.0, *MySpace* was it.

As technology progressed and Internet connections improved (e.g. increased speed), SNSs started to evolve into what are now referred to as OSM. Whereas SNSs emphasized – and still emphasize – *networking*, specifically, for instance through friend lists, the term OSM encompasses all social platforms regardless of the centrality given to networking, or, in other words, where the primary activity is not necessarily social networking exclusively. This is another key distinction, one that brings us back to Kaplan and Haenlein's definition of OSM. Whereas some authors choose the term SNSs to synonymously designate OSM (especially in less recent research), this is problematic because the literature suggests OSM is, in fact, the umbrella or generic term, while SNSs have a more specific function. The term OSM, as we have seen, refers to all kinds of online social media, *including* SNSs. In short, one of the more effective ways of categorizing and defining various OSM is by the type of UGC found on the platform itself. Some OSM platforms, for instance, showcase and emphasize the curation and sharing of visual content in the form of photos or videos (e.g. *Pinterest, Flickr, YouTube*), while others combine blogs and microblogs (e.g. *Twitter, Tumblr*), while still others enable users to upload an amalgamation of different UGC in 'permanent' (e.g. *Facebook, Instagram*) or 'non-permanent' ways (e.g. *SnapChat*)[2] (Desjardins 2010, 2011a, b, 2013a).

The popularity of OSM is expanding at an exponential pace. Web users are now more likely to access content via OSM as opposed to a more 'traditional' web search (cf. Wihbey 2014). In fact, a UM (Universal McCaan) Social Media Tracker Wave 5 report (2010) indicates that almost 75% of active Internet users regularly consult SNSs. A 2015 eMarketer report indicates that just under 20 million Canadians are expected to access social networks (social networks in this report appear to be defined as OSM) on at least a monthly basis, which is in line with rates seen in the United States. *Facebook* alone boasts nearly 1.59 billion monthly active users according to *Statista* (2016). *Instagram*, an OSM platform that enables users to upload and share photos and videos, now offers support for more than two dozen languages (Moscaritolo 2012), which suggests it has a global user-base and is popular.

This overview of OSM indicates not only the relationships between technological advancement and changes in communication trends (a theme Cronin explores in *Translation in the Digital Age*) and the rise of OSM as a dominant contemporary mediality, it also implicitly and explicitly suggests that OSM are here to stay, though this landscape may radically transform in years to come (boyd 2009). It is hoped that this brief overview contextualizes OSM for readers who may be less familiar with the development of OSM and the Web, more generally, and provides the definitions for the terms that will be used throughout the book. The evolution of OSM and TS do share some overlap, particularly with respect to how technological advancement has radically impacted human communication.

2.2 TS and OSM: An Overview

OSM has, to a limited degree, been addressed by a select group of researchers whose work focuses on translation, the Web, UGC, user-generated translation (UGT) and web localization. In the last 5 or so years, especially, there has been a rise in publications and conferences addressing new translation realities, which are largely the product of increased Web and OSM access. For instance, in an overview dedicated to addressing the state of TS 20 years after its 'linguistic emancipation', Snell-Hornby (2012) addresses the potential effects of technology and globalization on languages, and briefly alludes to some of the translation activity occurring on *Facebook*. Other researchers, such as Perrino (2009), Folaron (2010a, b, 2012), Pym (2011a, b), O'Hagan (2011), Cronin (2013), Bacalu (2013), to name but a few, have addressed how the Web and technology, more broadly, is impacting the field and the profession: from having created and given rise to translator networks to generating a collaborative and crowdsourced participatory translation culture. These researchers also appear to be in agreement in that the Web and OSM will continue to have a major impact for the profession and the field alike, hence the importance of pursuing research in this area.

The literature in TS on translation and OSM can be divided into six major categories[3]: (1) *crowdsourced or collaborative translation in connection with or on OSM platforms* (Kelly 2009; Perrino 2009; Schonfeld 2009; Costales 2011; Dolmaya 2011; O'Brien 2011); (2) *translation and OSM in relation to activism and political engagement* (Colón Rodriguez 2013; Baker 2015); (3) *translation, OSM and crisis management* (i.e. how humanitarian and aid services are leveraging translation across OSM to deliver important aid news or updates) (Sutherlin 2013; O'Brien 2016); (4) *best practices, how to's and codes of ethics* (Hamilton and Lavallée 2012); (5) *fan translation on OSM* (O'Hagan 2009); (6) *analyses of online crowdsourced translation versus other translation technologies (MT/CAT), with a particular focus on translation quality assessment* (TQA) (e.g. Anastasiou and Gupta 2011; García 2015; Jiménez-Crespo 2015).

2.2.1 Crowdsourced Translation/Collaborative Translation and OSM

The first category, crowdsourced and collaborative translation, is undoubtedly the most exhaustive area in which TS scholars have begun analysing OSM translation phenomena. First, there is much debate surrounding the terms 'crowdsourced' and 'collaborative'. O'Brien (2011) observes that *collaborative* translation is not a new phenomenon, and cites the Septuagint translation of the *Old Testament* as one historical example of how 70 translators 'collaborated' to produce a single target text. O'Brien further defines contemporary collaborative translation as translation activity that occurs between any two (or more) agents involved in the translation process, from the translators themselves, to clients, to editors, to publishers, to agencies and so on. Based on this definition, then, collaborative translation does not necessarily have to occur in an online setting; in fact, group translations done among a team of students in the classroom is a perfect 'analog' example. The term *crowdsourcing* (and by extension, crowdsourced translation), however, has a meaning that is more directly associated with the digital era. Howe (2006, 2008) coined the term 'crowdsourcing' in an article written for *Wired* magazine, a publication focusing on new technology and digital trends. To crowdsource essentially means to go beyond an in-house team or group of employees in order to 'assign' a specific task to the masses, in the hope of leveraging the 'crowd's' diverse experience and knowledge. Evidently, thanks to digital technologies and the Web, crowdsourcing, whether for altruistic or commercial purposes, is now easier than ever. Based on these definitions, collaborative translation and crowdsourced translation are not viewed here as synonymous, but rather, in some cases, as complementary.

OSM platforms such as *Facebook* and *Twitter* are used globally and constitute two of the most important examples of crowdsourced translation. Research done thus far in this area has focused on *Facebook*'s collaborative *and* crowdsourced translation project launched in 2007 (O'Brien 2011). By soliciting its 'crowd', that is the users of the platform, *Facebook* has been able to provide translations of its content in over 75 languages (Snell-Hornby 2012), and it hopes 'to support Facebook in the native language of all [its] users and people who want to use the site' (Abram 2008). Moreover, thanks to the Translate Facebook App; it is easy for 'translators all over the world' (Facebook 2016) to help with the project (interestingly, *Facebook* makes no mention of *professional* translators and seems to label all translation contributors 'translators' – an issue that will be further addressed in Chap. 3). *Facebook* now also offers the option of having UGC (newsfeed items, primarily) translated automatically and in real-time based on a user's language preferences. *Twitter*'s crowdsourcing initiatives follow a similar model (i.e. soliciting the user-base to assist in translation efforts), thanks to its Translation Centre. The Translation Centre allows users to translate content based on a set of guidelines, which includes language-specific glossaries. At the time of writing, *Twitter* supports 48 languages and is constantly working to add more, notably by using the @translator account to post calls for translators who might be able to assist in languages that aren't currently available.

Researchers in TS have also focused on how crowdsourcing is impacting professional translation (and the translation industry more generally) with specific attention paid to remuneration, recognition and collaboration between stakeholders. While these areas are certainly worth investigation, some gaps have been identified, two of which are dealt with below.

First, TS research on OSM and crowdsourced translation focuses predominantly on the translation of the platforms themselves (or platform-produced content, for instance FAQs, or user guidelines, or community rules) rather than on the translation of the UGC, although this is slowly changing, for instance, with *Facebook* now offering real-time MT to translate newsfeed items. This gap raises two issues. The first issue is that the linguistic adaptation of these OSM platforms for 'new' language markets is essentially a form of localization, and, thus, not a wholly new topic for TS research – that is, if we agree that research in localization can be subsumed within the larger scope of TS. In other words, research on localization could be applicable in this context and, therefore, discussions surrounding *how* these platforms are translated might not generate novel insights. Here, however, the significant distinction is that instead of an in-house translation team, it is the *Facebook* community ('crowd') that produces most of the translation work – and this, it would seem, should be where TS focuses its attention, perhaps by profiling a sample population of the 'translator crowd' to see what type of competencies these individuals possess and how many of them have formal translation experience (data that could form the basis for developments in translator training for the digital era). The second issue is that research that focuses on the crowdsourcing of the platform's translation largely obfuscates other forms of equally significant OSM translation activity, for instance, self-translation (cf. Grutman 2009) of UGC done by individual *Facebook* users or hybrid posts combining iconographic languages (e.g. *Emoji*) and natural languages, which are rather compelling example of intersemiotic translation. It is in this regard that Perrino's (2009) concept of 'user-generated translation' is particularly noteworthy: unlike crowdsourced translation, which generally mimics a professional translation model in which a brief is posted by a client requesting the participation of translators (e.g. *Facebook* calling upon its community of users to help translate the platform and site content), UGT can be done at any point, on any platform, whether there is a brief or not. Perrino (*ibid.*) defines UGT as a form of translation that harnesses Web 2.0 technologies, applications and platforms to make UGC (or online content, more generally) available and accessible in a variety of languages.[4] Though the UGT definition Perrino proposes coincides more generally with definitions of crowdsourced translation suggested by other scholars, the suggestion here is that UGT can more readily encompass translation activity that is prompted and motivated by the *users* themselves (i.e. translation of *their own* content, *their* UGC, by *themselves*, based on *their* understanding of what 'good' or 'effective' translation might be). This definition offers a different way of framing OSM translation phenomena, one that is more user-centred rather than focused on the community or the crowd. Crowd-focused research in TS is undoubtedly important, but users' self-translations of UGC could offer more insight into why some individuals feel compelled or motivated to translate their content on their own terms, without the prompt of OSM platforms (or client briefs, for that matter). Moreover, user-focused analyses have the potential to disrupt the assumption that crowdsourced models are based on a 'bottom-up' approach that is supposedly more 'democratic'. When we consider that *Facebook* is operated by Facebook Inc. – a transnational corporation – is the call for crowdsourced translation truly democratic and ethical, or is it merely a disguised form of free labour? Are translators now willing to be remunerated in the form of *likes* for the sake of making *Facebook* more linguistically accessible? These questions indicate the need to consider how social media is impacting the economy, the language services industry as well as what this means for professional translators.

In addition, the corpus of analysed OSM platforms needs to be broadened. While *Facebook* and *Twitter* are the two most frequently discussed platforms (*Facebook* is mentioned more often than any other platform in the surveyed literature, for instance, in the work of O'Brien [2011], Snell-Hornby [2012], Costales [2011] and Desjardins [2013a]), it is important to consider how other newer and increasingly popular platforms are addressing the issue of translation, be it through crowdsourced initiatives or other models. Thus far, there is a dearth of material in TS discussing platforms such as *Instagram* and *SnapChat*, two increasingly popular photo-sharing OSM platforms (Van Grove 2013). Though OSM engagement across platforms is steady or rising, studies suggest that *Facebook*'s overall popularity is either waning, especially among younger generations opting to converge on other sites, or reaching a saturation point in specific markets (Morris 2013). How does translation occur on these other OSM platforms and sites? Is the crowdsourced model standard across most OSM platforms or are other platforms opting for other translation strategies?

2.2.2 *Translation, Activism and OSM*

The second category linking OSM and TS comprises research that considers how OSM are being leveraged in political, civic and activist translation efforts. The reviewed literature indicates that OSM are generally viewed as an aid against censorship, a way of combatting-biased media or redressing power imbalances within news journalism and a means to reach the masses (i.e. a form of citizen journalism that aims to reach all, not only an educated elite). OSM do effectively play a significant role in activist translation movements. Thanks to the English translations of the *Printemps Érable* movement in Canada, for instance, the country's

English-speaking provinces were made aware of student grievances in primarily French-speaking Québec. OSM was crucial in affording a tool for reaching Anglophone audiences in this particular case study, as many local newspapers outside of Québec did not initially consider this movement of much significance. Despite increasing momentum in this area, one aspect of OSM and activist translation that has yet to receive additional attention is that of whether or not online activism is really effective. While the *Printemps Érable* constitutes a good example of activist translation being successful in disseminating information to a larger audience and providing a counterpoint to mainstream Anglophone coverage in provinces other than Québec (and even English-language publications within Québec), other activist initiatives have not always been successful in engaging audiences in any sort of tangible manner. Morozov (2009, online; 2010; 2013), for instance, suggests that a lot of UGC and OSM activity that might appear to be activist in intent is in fact illusory and constitutes 'feel-good online activism that has zero political impact or social impact'. Moreover, he adds: 'It gives those who participate in "slacktivist" campaigns an illusion of having meaningful impact on the world without demanding anything more than joining a Facebook group' (*ibid.*). However, in TS, it has been argued that translation efforts seeking to provide content in minority languages or to revert power imbalances are generally laudable (UNESCO 2009) and are anything but 'slacktivism'. In fact, translation on OSM platforms can serve to fight against censorship and oppressive regimes (Baker 2006, 2015). But, the question deserves further investigation: are there cases where translation does not benefit activist causes or where translation only fulfils a superficial role? For instance, in Canada, where there is an official languages policy, the *Official Languages Act* (1988), translation might at times be performed only to obtain funding (though never stated as such) and to appease outcries among – usually Francophone – minorities. Could we envision situations in which activist translation is part of what Morozov calls 'feel-good activism' (2009, online)? For instance, in the case of the *Printemps Érable*, the 'translators' who translated the media coverage and posted it onto *Tumblr* were not jeopardizing their lives or raising funds or providing on-the-ground aid. Though these translators certainly helped in creating more balanced coverage of the events that took place in Québec in 2012, which is a way of countering biased media, one could ask whether or not these translation efforts resulted in any more or less sympathy from the Anglophone audiences for which the translations were intended.

Dissent Magazine published an article discussing the Anglophone reaction as ranging from 'indifference' to 'puzzlement' (Fraenkel and Etinson 2012, online), which supports the hypothesis that translation may not have succeeded in modifying perceptions of the student protests among Anglophone audiences. From a critical perspective, the issue of 'slacktivism' or 'feel-good activism' is therefore another related area that warrants further investigation. What types of actions or consequences must OSM activist translation generate to constitute more than superficial engagement? Is activist translation on OSM always a 'good' thing? Can there be insidious motivations? How is such activism received?

2.2.3 Translation, Crisis Management and OSM

In the third area of study, scholars have addressed how OSM and Web technologies can be used in crisis management, for instance, by disseminating information quickly about natural disasters, humanitarian efforts, fundraising and victim statistics. Unlike UGC and UGT that fulfils a largely social or entertainment function, UGC and UGT produced in a crisis context represents an entirely different set of challenges and raises a number of different, but equally pressing questions. As Sutherlin (2013) indicates, crowdsourced translation in a crisis setting has significant implications that can, at best, provide a cost-effective and near-immediate means for the dissemination of information or, at worst, contribute to inaccurate reporting which can have an immediate impact on loss of human life. She argues that crowdsourcing is not necessarily an optimal model for translation in crisis contexts and supports her argument using four crisis examples. Sutherlin demonstrates that in a crisis situation, individuals who create UGC, for instance *tweets* (140-character micro-blogs published on *Twitter*), might be themselves the victims of the crisis. Translation of this specific UGC, then, Sutherlin hypothesizes, does not necessarily benefit the victims; rather, translation would serve to inform *other* stakeholders, such as the press, governmental agencies and emergency services. She argues that in order for crowdsourced translation to be more effective, it would have to operate according to a two-way or recursive loop model, in which translation acts as an intermediary for *both* the victims and the outside stakeholders. In this manner, information about aid relief or safety measures could be relayed back to the victims themselves. In turn, these victims could then give a ground-zero assessment of whether the relief measures are effective or not. She also stresses some of the problems associated with the use of automatic machine translation embedded within OSM platforms in crisis situations. Although the intent is to spread information in two or more languages rapidly, automatic machine translation applications, such as *Google Translate*, tend to homogenize target output – cultural contexts, dialect variants, non-verbal or visual cues are ignored – leading to an incomplete picture or creating potential misunderstandings that only worsen the crisis situation. Sutherlin emphasizes the need to learn from previous crises in order to develop more accountable forms of translation in these types of urgent situations. As she indicates, up until now, the focus appeared to be on translating for quantity (i.e. more information) and not quality. Could application developers work more closely with cross-cultural experts and professional translators to create more adequate translation models? As an interdisciplinary field, TS must go beyond disciplines in the humanities and social sciences to fields such as computer engineering, computer science and informatics, to offer insights to those developing crowdsourcing technologies. Moreover, the longer-lasting implications of crisis translation(s) on OSM must be assessed; when policies are based on content that has been translated in haste and in exceptional circumstances, and sometimes by an emotional and inexperienced 'crowd', are the bases for these policies truly sound? Who becomes accountable for inaccurate or mistranslated OSM content in crisis contexts? Sutherlin's work has paved the way for the analysis of other crisis cases in which crowdsourcing, translation and OSM interact at crossroads of disaster and hope (cf. Federici 2016).

2.2.4 Professional Translation, Best Practices and OSM

Although it has been said that TS has evolved beyond the linguistic paradigm, OSM have brought about new linguistic realities (for instance, limited character counts, the use of hashtags, and lexical choices that contribute to search engine optimization[5] [SEO]) that have implications for interlinguistic translation. In this sense, perhaps OSM is favouring a return to linguistics in TS (Snell-Hornby 2006). Comparative analyses of translated social media content have provided templates for professional translators working in this area. As corporations, smaller businesses and even politicians and celebrities seek to create an online *presence*, they turn to translation as a way of communicating their brand to larger audiences (Oswald 2012). Now, whether this UGC is translated by users (UGT), crowdsourced or automatically translated depends largely on available human and financial resources. But regardless of the model used to bring about translated content, the fact remains that very few resources exist for professional translators looking to refine their OSM translation skills. For instance, the in-house translation teams at *Library and Archives Canada* and at the *Royal College of Physicians and Surgeons of Canada*[6] use MT to assist in the translation of OSM-specific content, yet both teams underscore the lack of more 'traditional' tools, such as dictionaries or manuals that offer pragmatic solutions for translating challenging *tweets* or *status updates.* At the time of writing, one of the most comprehensive (and only?) 'how-to' manuals for professional translators working with UGC requiring human translation expertise (as is the case with the social media content that both *Library and Archives Canada* and *The Royal College of Physician and Surgeons of Canada* produce) is *Tweets et gazouillis: pour des traductions qui chantent* (2012), by Grant Hamilton and François Lavallée, a pair of prominent Canadian certified translators. In their book, Hamilton and Lavallée have reproduced a corpus of 1,750 bilingual *tweets.* The corpus serves as the basis for tips and tricks meant to help translators find effective and fluent solutions regardless of the constraints posed by OSM (spatial, temporal, lexical, etc.). Though many professional translation blogs, translator forums and language forums address the various challenges posed by the translation of OSM content and UGC more specifically, these types of online references are again a form of 'crowd' knowledge – one that has not necessarily been vetted or informed by professional or institutional insight. Accreditation, professional experience and institutional credentials are not necessarily a guarantee of higher quality translation, a fact underscored by the very act of crowdsourcing in which non-professional translators have been shown to translate adequately and efficiently. That said, reference materials based on quantitative and qualitative OSM translation data can serve 'crowd' translators and in-house professionals alike by functioning as a sort of 'recipe' book with strategies and solutions for overcoming fundamental interlinguistic translation challenges, such as lexical equivalence, cultural adaptation and concision. Unfortunately, it would seem references of this nature, whether in analog (manual) or virtual form (blog; forum), often pair two dominant languages (usually English and another language) as opposed to exploring the translation of UGC in other, less pervasive language combinations. This could be the result of English being the *lingua franca* on OSM, in which the translation flow is usually *from* English *into* another language, though more robust research would be needed to support this hypothesis. In any case, vetted material offering solutions and strategies for effective UGC translation would be welcome for translator training and education. If more of these materials were to become available, codes of ethics and best practices could come to the forefront and thus inform all areas of OSM translation.

2.2.5 *Crowdsourced Translation, Fan Translation and OSM*

Web 2.0 and OSM have also had implications for fan culture. Whereas fans of various media products such as films, television series or games once had limited means of interacting with one another and rarely influenced product development from inception onwards, the landscape has now changed. In a comprehensive survey of game localization and fan studies, O'Hagan and Mangiron (2013) address how fan culture has shifted from a more passive paradigm to a very active and participatory culture (Jenkins 2006, 2008). The Web has afforded fans of games, films, television series and other media a means by which to engage with content in unprecedented ways. Initially, fansubbing, fandubbing and translating were a form of fan engagement that could have significant legal implications. This can still be the case, although some game companies are now more open to the idea of soliciting their fans' input, notably by leveraging their enthusiasm and interest to crowdsource the translation of their products, often at a lesser cost/delay and sometimes with better results (i.e. translations that please the audiences and fan-bases of other geographic locales), a point Drugan (2013, p.173) alludes to. After all, who better to translate these games than the hardcore gamers (who may happen to be elite bilinguals) who know the games and genre best? Fan pages on *Facebook*, *Tumblr* fan blogs and UGC uploaded to *YouTube* (e.g. fansubbed or fandubbed UGT) would all constitute excellent empirical and qualitative case studies from which TS could benefit. Unfortunately, this area largely escapes the scope of this book, but O'Hagan and Mangiron have certainly touched upon an increasingly important niche. In the years to come, it is likely that game localization and mobile application translation will represent a large market segment of the translation and localization industry.

2.2.6 *TQA and OSM*

The sixth and final area in which TS research has incorporated OSM is that of TQA in comparative analyses involving online automatic machine translation (*Google Translate* being one of the more popular examples), crowdsourced translation and other forms of machine translation. According to Anastasiou and Gupta (2011, p. 637), crowdsourcing and machine translation share a few similarities: they can cope with 'high volume, perform at high speed, and reduce translation cost'. Anastasiou and Gupta (2011) compare various translation workflow models and in so doing, address the issue of quality (i.e. what combination of translation workflow models produces the most optimal output). They conclude that more 'traditional' models involving MT and translation memory (TM) should now also incorporate crowdsourcing: 'MT, TM, and generally automatic translation research should take the crowdsourcing translation phenomenon seriously and try to embrace it [. . .] Only then can the ideal triangle with low cost, and high speed and quality be feasible' (*ibid.*: 654). However, as previously discussed, the increased push for crowdsourced, low-cost and high-speed translation solutions has significant repercussions for the profession and for the training of translators. It would be valuable to see if there exists a generational divide among younger generations of translators (who might be more keen to be 'symbolically remunerated') and older generations in relation to their perceptions of crowdsourcing. If the new economy is being shaped by social media, as Fuchs (2014, 2015) argues, then perhaps translators of all generations will have to accept crowdsourcing as the new workflow model and embrace new forms of recognition and remuneration. Also, the definition of 'quality' in this context will need to be examined. When the crowd provides the output in lieu of a single individual translator, it then becomes more challenging for revisers or supervisors to address and amend poor output, unless strategies and tools are put in place to facilitate interaction with the crowd. Is quality then determined by the end-product? The efficiency of the crowd to produce rapid solutions? The degree of collaboration achieved to produce the output (which incidentally supposes that more involvement rather than less is better in the translation process)?

2.3 Conclusion

This overview was intended to identify the body of work within TS that has addressed OSM, whether head-on or peripherally. The review suggests that crowdsourcing, in all of its manifestations, has been a forefront topic in studying the relationships between Web 2.0 and translation. Undoubtedly, crowdsourcing has radical implications for translation and TS, some of which will be further discussed in the following chapters. However, this book will also seek to address areas that have been significantly or entirely neglected, for instance the UGT of UGC that is *not* the result of a call for crowdsourcing, but rather that is individually motivated (here, the concept of self-translation becomes all the more relevant); the imperative need for intersemiotic translation given the pervasiveness of newer hypervisual OSM platforms and the increased reliance on artificial iconographic languages such as *Emoji*; and the relevance of including OSM literacy in translator training. Hopefully, these additional insights will contribute to filling some of the gaps identified in this chapter. This overview of existing TS literature references primarily English-language scholarship, which in turn could result in an unintentional omission of non-English scholarship. In this regard, research involving other language combinations or OSM platforms restricted to non-English markets would be greatly welcomed.

Notes

1. Fuchs (2014) provides a comprehensive list of 'social media' definitions curated from various social media experts; though he does not list Kaplan and Haenlein's definition, their definition does comprise many of the traits outlined by other authors.
2. UGC uploaded onto sites like *Facebook* and *Twitter* are permanently recorded and available to their intended audiences; in other words, they remain 'posted' on the OSM platform, unless the user who uploaded the content chooses to delete it or make it temporarily unavailable. *SnapChat* differs in that content uploaded to its servers is only made available to an intended audience for a limited period of time (anywhere from 1 s to 24 h), after which *SnapChat* claims it deletes the content permanently from its servers.
3. There are undoubtedly singular case studies that might examine other aspects of translation and OSM that are not covered by these six categories. These six overarching categories reflect the areas in which there has been enough research produced to warrant either encyclopaedic entries in references such as *The Handbook of Translation Studies, The Oxford Handbook of Translation Studies*; special thematic issues of peer-reviewed journals, for instance *Linguistica Antverpiensia's* special issue on *Translation as a Social Activity: Community Translation 2.0.*
4. O'Hagan (2009) also uses the term UGT in her work, but does not make Perrino's (2009) distinction with regard to who initiates the translation (a call for translation by corporate entities, for instance, versus individually

motivated UGT). She also seems to imply that UGT is synonymous with collaborative initiatives, which is not the view taken here.

5. "Search engine optimization (SEO) refers to methods used to increase traffic to a website by increasing its search engine page rank. SEO often involves improving the quality of the content, ensuring that it is rich in relevant keywords and organizing it by using subheads, bullet points, and bold and italic characters. SEO also ensures that the site's HTML is optimized such that a search engine can determine what is on the page and display it as a search result in relevant searches. These standards involve the use of metadata, including the title tag and meta description. Cross linking within the website is also important" (Technopedia 2016d).
6. These examples are given based on personal, first-hand experience working as a professional translator at the *Royal College of Physician and Surgeons of Canada* and as a bilingual Communications Office/Social Media at *Library and Archives Canada*.

CHAPTER 3

Translation and Social Media: In Theory

Abstract Chapter 3 considers how online social media (OSM) can impact the theorization of translation, translation practices and concepts (i.e. *in theory*). The chapter starts with an analysis of the changes in human communicational behaviour that have been brought on or exacerbated by OSM. This chapter also looks how language is changing or, rather, adapting to the social media landscape (e.g. increased use of visual content; the paradigmatic nature of hashtags; the rise of *Emoji*). Consideration is also given to 'play labour' and the 'like' economy and what these might mean for translator remuneration and recognition. The concept of 'augmentation' (Davenport and Kirby, *Harvard Business Review* 93(6):59–65, 2015) is also examined and presented as a lens with which to approach and reframe the 'threat' of crowdsourced translation and translation automation.

Keywords Human communicational behaviour · Language · Visual content · Paradigmatic · Hashtags · *Emoji* · Play labour · 'Like' economy · Translator remuneration · Recognition · Augmentation · Crowdsourced translation · Automation

3.1 Introduction

Building on Carr's (2008, 2010) work on the topic of how the Web is radically changing communicational and behavioural patterns, Vandendorpe's (1999, 2009) insights on reading, interactivity and the visual, as well as

R. Desjardins, *Translation and Social Media*, Palgrave Studies in Translating and Interpreting, DOI 10.1057/978-1-137-52255-9_3

Charron's (2005) argument that translation is now a 'zero-time' process (which intersects with some of Fuchs' [2014, 2015] work), this chapter offers a critical, albeit different, take on some of the implications of online social media (OSM) and user-generated content (UGC) for translation studies (TS). The idea is to explore how OSM and UGC are impacting translation beyond existing debates on crowdsourcing, as some of the introductory statements and examples have suggested. Through the exploration of some of the theoretical connections between translation and OSM, the intent is to build on existing translation theory to account for some of the newer realities brought on by OSM and the digital era. By identifying and building upon relevant theoretical concepts, it then becomes easier to inform translator training (Chap. 4) and professional practice (Chap. 5).

3.2 Technology, OSM and Change in Human Communicational Behaviour

Can technology shape or modify human behaviour and communication? More specifically, can Web 2.0 technologies shape or modify translation behaviour or behaviours towards translation? As Littau (2011, 2015), Cronin (2013) and Standage (2013) have shown with other forms of 'analogue' social media, the evolution of technology can indeed impact how communication occurs, in turn shaping human behaviour. For instance, thanks to the near omnipresence of broadband wireless connectivity (WiFi) in economically developed countries, the increased uptake in mobile technology and increased access to the Web (Akamai 2014), we are never further than a few clicks away or a swipe away from retrieving much of the information we wish to obtain. The instantaneous nature of information retrieval as well as its accessibility, some opine, has created a society in which patience, imagination, attention spans and face-to-face human interaction are all impacted. For instance, Nicholas Carr (2008, 2010), an American journalist who has written for *Wired* (among other publications), readily discusses how Web 2.0 has markedly changed his own behaviour in an article published in *The Atlantic* (Carr 2008, online):

> Over the past few years I've had an uncomfortable sense that someone, or something, has been tinkering with my brain, remapping the neural circuitry, reprogramming the memory. My mind isn't going–so far as I can tell–but it's changing. [...] I think I know what's going on. For more than a

decade now, I've been spending a lot of time online, searching, and surfing and sometimes adding to the great databases of the Internet.

Carr uses his personal experience as a springboard to discuss more generalized trends pertaining to human behaviour and communication. He argues that while the Web has been a 'boon' for researchers and writers especially, notably by facilitating near-instant fact-checking and referencing, humans are no longer 'thinking the way they used to think' (*ibid.*). In the same article, Carr also revisits the influential work of Marshall McLuhan (1964) to support his thesis: '[. . .] media are not just passive channels of information. They supply the stuff of thought' (*ibid.*).

In a similar vein, although with less attention given to the Web specifically and more emphasis given to the effects of technology on language, Pym (2011a, p. 1) follows a line of thought that runs parallel to Carr's. Pym posits that technology 'extends the ways we interact with the world: our arms, our sight, our capacity to hear, touch, to move over distance'. Pym further argues that communication technologies (such as the Web and OSM platforms, although he never explicitly mentions either) have a significant impact on translation, notably by extending the possibilities for cross-cultural contact. However, digging deeper into how communication technologies might impact *how* translators carry out the *process* of translation, Pym makes the case that memory is the human faculty most affected by the pervasiveness of electronic and readily accessible content and that this can complicate translators' decision-making. The connection with OSM and crowdsourcing, here, is evident: given the increasing abundance of online translator networks (both professional and volunteer), such as *ProZ* (ProZ.com), online databases (term banks such as Canada's *Termium*, for instance), online automatic machine translation applications (e.g. *Google Translate*) and the option of soliciting the 'crowd', translators now have more resources than ever before. This, as Pym asserts, can be an impediment to efficient translation, as translators are confronted with ever-expanding lists of solutions and alternatives making decisiveness more challenging. Whereas a bilingual paper dictionary might have offered one or two decontextualized solutions, the Web and the communication it enables, multiplies the possibilities. There is no denying, then, that technology impacts translator behaviour.

In an infographic that provocatively suggests a connection between OSM and psychopathic tendencies ('Is Social Media Making . . . ', n.d.), a juxtaposition of the pros and cons of technology on human behaviour is made – and while Carr (2008) and Pym (2011a) both address the relationship between digital technology and human (translator) behaviour in a broader manner, this specific infographic presents behavioural changes/trends and OSM data exclusively. According to the infographic data, which was compiled from various sources including *Business Insider* ('Is Social Media Making...', n.d.), avid social media users are more inclined to lie, to be antisocial, to be egocentric and to exhibit poor behavioural control. And even though the validity of this data certainly warrants further scientific assessment, the fact that the fifth edition of the *Diagnostic Statistical Manual* (DSM-V) now lists Internet disorders (e.g. Internet addiction) among its pages does lend some weight to a connection between disordered behaviour and avid – or more specifically, addictive – social media usage.[1] Could a connection be made here with these problematic behavioural trends and translation activity on OSM platforms? Do those who contribute to the crowdsourced translation of OSM platforms possess these tendencies? And what would be the consequences if so? While obtaining data to answer these questions would be challenging, this is an area worthy of scrutiny, particularly as research into cognitive studies and TS delves deeper into translator behaviour. When we consider how translation has the power to disseminate, but to also censor or skew information (Kuhiwczak 2011; Baer et al. 2012), and when information is increasingly spread through OSM platforms,[2] there should be concern that some of the UGT contributors (whether crowdsourcers or laypeople who are OSM users) might espouse these behavioural tendencies. Bilingual OSM users have the power to translate UGC in the ways they see fit, and when this falls outside of more regimented modes of crowdsourcing (such as those used by OSM platforms such as *Facebook* and *Twitter*), there is no assurance of quality, accuracy or ethical practice.

Let us consider a *Facebook* user who decides to partially translate a news report as part of a status update or UGC post. This user is not a formally trained or credentialed translator. Let us assume, for the sake of the example, that their 'friends' list (i.e. the user's *Facebook* network) primarily comprises unilingual speakers. We could then imagine, in this scenario, that the user might shift some of the nuances, adapt the content, first by decontextualizing it from the original source and then by cropping it to fit the status word allowance and to fit an agenda. While this hypothetical example does not significantly differ[3] from an in-person conversation, in which a bilingual individual might report a news story to a unilingual friend, the important distinction here is the *viral* nature of OSM content and the repercussions viral content can create. Unlike the in-person conversation between friends that may never reach other audiences, and unlike the individual who consults news online on a reputable news website, but never takes action beyond reading the news story,[4] the person who posts UGC on social media can see their content rapidly 'move' from user to user, audience to audience. Viral dissemination of UGC is one of the characteristics of OSM and it is defined as 'the passing of content between individuals through networks' (Wihbey 2014, p. 6). When users produce their own content or disseminate content they've translated on OSM, they multiply the potential readers of that content, thus potentially increasing the viral factor of the post (and this is especially the case for profiles that are public, i.e. accessible and open to the wider Internet population). Here, translation is a significant social vector: a unilingual post might reach one linguistic audience, but a translated one now has the potential to 'reach' (a term often used when gauging online engagement) at least two. In other words, the more UGC is translated by users (to recall: this is not crowdsourcing but rather, individuals translating their own UGC), the more the odds are favourable for this content to spread quickly, that is become viral. Thus, translation has a multiplying property on OSM.

If this line of thought is connected to some of the aforementioned behavioural patterns (i.e. behavioural tendencies), it might be worth investigating how translation (UGT, more specifically) can be leveraged by individuals wishing to disseminate specific forms of UGC over others to fit an agenda. Users can use translation to falsify or skew information; they can use it to spread information that may be primarily beneficial to them, with the illusion of wanting to make content available for speakers of different languages. For instance, this is sometimes the case with individuals looking to create and promote their own brands or products. In some cases, it might be possible to imagine that users would feel compelled to translate UGC in haste, especially when UGC is related to a time-sensitive event or news item, for instance, a terrorist attack or natural disaster). Although the act of translating may have been done in haste and without much consideration to the effects, this may not necessarily be indicative of poor behavioural control on behalf of the translator. But tracking this kind of online behaviour and translation on OSM will likely supplement research on the topic of human behaviour, social media and language analysis (cf. Sumner et al. 2012). One way then in which TS can greatly contribute to social media studies is by underscoring how translation is not an innocuous act; OSM users who may demonstrate even psychopathic tendencies online could be using translation in insidious ways, for instance, by spreading violent or terrorist ideologies and manifestos.[5] As OSM is increasingly used to mobilize users around social, political and ideological issues, research merging insights on terrorism studies, TS, social psychology and social media studies provides an interdisciplinary framework with which to better understand how radical movements gain momentum on OSM and how translation acts as a vector in these contexts.

3.3 Establishing Links Between OSM and Translation: Laying the Groundwork

The shifts in how we communicate – from how we read and write, to how we process information – which have been brought on by the Web and, now, increasingly OSM, are significant for translation and translation theory. Yet, the literature on this topic, beyond crowdsourcing, is limited. Though Cronin's recent publications *Translation and Globalization* (2003) and *Translation in the Digital Age* (2013) have contributed significantly to development in this area, he does not tackle OSM specifically, nor does Pym (2011a) in his discussion of the impact technology has on translation, and nor does Munday (2016) in his discussion of 'New Media'. Chapter 2 outlined the current literature connecting OSM and translation and revealed that recent scholarship tends to focus on how OSM platforms are translated through different crowdsourcing models. However, crowdsourcing has posed ethical dilemmas with regard to translation remuneration, visibility and translation flows, that is, which languages are being translated from and into, themes that are explored in greater detail by McDonough Dolmaya (2011). These questions, those that link critical theory, translation theory and OSM, are those that will be further developed in this chapter. Most of the crowdsourced translation applications available today are part of OSM platforms and sites, and social media management and monitoring tools (SMM)[6] (e.g. social media platforms such as *Facebook, Twitter, LinkedIn* and SMM tools, such as *Facebook Insights, HootSuite, Salesforce Radian6, Oracle Social Cloud*, etc.[7]) are, therefore, in some cases, developed by the very corporations that own the OSM platform (Dolmaya 2011; Fuchs 2015). As McDonough Dolmaya indicates, the corporate entities that are behind many of today's dominant OSM platforms have a vested interest in keeping their platforms profitable, which most users tend to mistake as being synonymous with accessible. OSM applications developed to facilitate the crowdsourced translation of OSM platforms (e.g. *Twitter, Facebook*) may seem to cater to diverse linguistic and cultural communities (i.e. the 'crowd'), but this is inaccurate, at best, and illusory, at worst. The implicit motivation for translating the *Facebook* or *Twitter* platform, for instance, is more likely to be corporate profit than ensuring that the platform be accessible for linguistically and culturally diverse audiences, despite promotional claims that indicate otherwise (Costales 2011, Dolmaya 2011). Fuchs (2015, p. 108) explains this using the concept of unpaid labour time:

> A specific way of increasing profits is to transform paid into unpaid labour time. Unpaid labour time has traditionally been present in the household, where houseworkers in social, emotional, affective, and physical labour reproduce labour power. [...] The examples of fast food restaurants, IKEA furniture assembled at home and self-service gas stations show that presumption (consumption that is productive and creating economic value and commodities) is not entirely new. The rise of the Internet and social media has amplified and extended this tendency. This emergence has intensified the historical trend that the boundaries between play and labour, work time and leisure time, production and consumption, the factory and the household, public and private life tend to blur.

The fact that *Facebook*, for instance, is accessible to an increasing number of linguistic and cultural audiences is far more likely to benefit corporate profit than anything else. And yet, OSM users willingly partake in unpaid labour time. If certified and volunteer translators *willingly* collaborate in the crowdsourcing of OSM platform translation, do they do so knowing that the profits do not go into their pockets? For an older generation of translators, those trained prior to the advent of the Internet and widespread use of OSM, the notion of 'giving away' translation for free hit a nerve. In 2009, the professional networking site and OSM platform *LinkedIn* invited its members (some of whom, it should be mentioned, had paid for their premium accounts) to assess interest in the platform's translation. None of the incentives proposed in return for the translation work were of a monetary nature (Dolmaya 2011), suggesting however implicitly or explicitly that translation was not worth the capital investment. Of course, this led to a vociferous debate in the *LinkedIn* translation community and beyond, where professional translators 't[ook] offence to being asked to volunteer to translate' (*ibid.*, p. 97) for a commercial entity (cf. 'Translators against Crowdsourcing by Commercial Businesses', 2015). Certainly, the idea that translation should be 'given away' or 'free' simply to make things more accessible is dubious; based on this argument, one could easily make the case that lawyers and medical doctors, or any other professional for that matter, should equally offer their services *pro bono* in the name of greater access. And while some professional volunteer organizations do exactly that, for instance, *Doctors Without Borders* and *Translators Without Borders*, we should be mindful that here the difference lies with who is commissioning the work. In *Without Borders* organizations, it is understood that the work conducted is done in a not-for-profit context, a point McDonough Dolmaya (*ibid.*) also addresses. In contrast, OSM platforms do not call for work to be done on a not-for-profit basis; it is quite the opposite, in fact.

However, what can be said of a new generation of translators: those brought up as 'digital natives' (Prensky 2001) and for whom symbolic remuneration in the form of social media validation (*Facebook 'likes'; Twitter 'favourites'; Instagram 'followers'*; and '*regrams*') might be as rewarding as the traditional paycheque? If we are to critically assess how OSM is impacting the translation industry and the power relations within it, we must consider the possibility that some translators (even across generational divides) might be willing to accept new forms of remuneration, an idea that will be further developed in Sect. 3.5 in relation to the 'like economy'. Ethnographic studies of millennial or 'digital native' translators and how they leverage social media as well as the 'like economy' would constitute a welcome contribution.

3.4 #Translation: Revisiting Intersemiotic Translation, *Lingua Francas* and Textuality

In the mid-twentieth century to about the 1980s, translation was still largely the focus of comparative literature or language departments (Snell-Hornby 2006; Brisset 2010), and it was usually defined as being an interlinguistic operation, between two (traditionally defined) languages, where 'equivalence' was measured in how 'faithful' a source text (ST) was to its target text (TT). Word choices were scrutinized and hypotheses were made as to what the original author's intent may or may not have been. Thinking on translation has made significant strides since this period, with various 'turns' (Snell-Hornby 2006; Long 2012) reshaping and redefining translation (Tymoczko 2006). In theorizing translation processes and practices, it is generally recognized that what is now translated are not words or texts, but discourse, that is a constellation of significations that are not bound by the constraints of the written word or printed page and that impact, and are impacted by, various social agents. Definitions of translation have been revisited throughout the twentieth century (e.g. Jakobson's [1959/2004] *intralingual translation; interlinguistic translation*; and *intersemiotic translation*) and broadened, such that now research on cultural translation (cf. Young 2003; Simon 2006; Brisset 2010), intersemiotic translation (cf. Cattrysse 2001; Tymoczko 2007; Desjardins 2008; Torresi 2008) and audiovisual/multimodal translation (Munday 2004; Gambier 2006; Taylor 2013), to name only these 'wider-ranging' examples, is now seen as integral to the field. Moreover, newer technology affords different forms and understandings of textuality. Whereas images and other semiotic modes (Kress and van Leeuwen 2006) might have once been disassociated from the source material requiring translation,[8] the multimodal nature of OSM and UGC make intersemiotic convergence inescapable; as Zappavigna (2012, p. 2) states: 'the advent of social media, technology that aims to support ambient interpersonal connection, has placed new and interesting semiotic pressure on language'. Kress and Van Leeuwen (2001, p. 20) define multimodality as 'the use of several semiotic modes in the design of a semiotic product or event'. Traditional media, including audiovisual media such as television programmes and printed advertisements, are equally, and have always been, multimodal, but research linking this line of thought to translation is relatively recent. Taylor (2013, p. 98) explains that 'multimodality [. . .] is not a new field of study in that everything to some extent is multimodal, but in the modern world, archetypal multimodal texts such as films, television programmes and websites, have greatly broadened the scope of such studies'.

UGC found on OSM can be defined as a 'semiotic product or event', in line with the definition proposed by Kress and Van Leeuwen. As such, when thinking about translation of social media content – whether user-generated or not – one must not only consider the content to be translated as a 'text' based on the interlinguistic (verbal) definition of translation (Desjardins 2013b), but also as discourse (i.e. part of a social constellation), and as a multimodal entity. As an example, let us consider a fictional[9] UGC post on the increasingly popular photo-sharing OSM platform *Instagram* (Fig. 3.1).

When a user posts UGC on *Instagram* it *must* include a photo; a user may then choose to add a caption, which is usually presented using

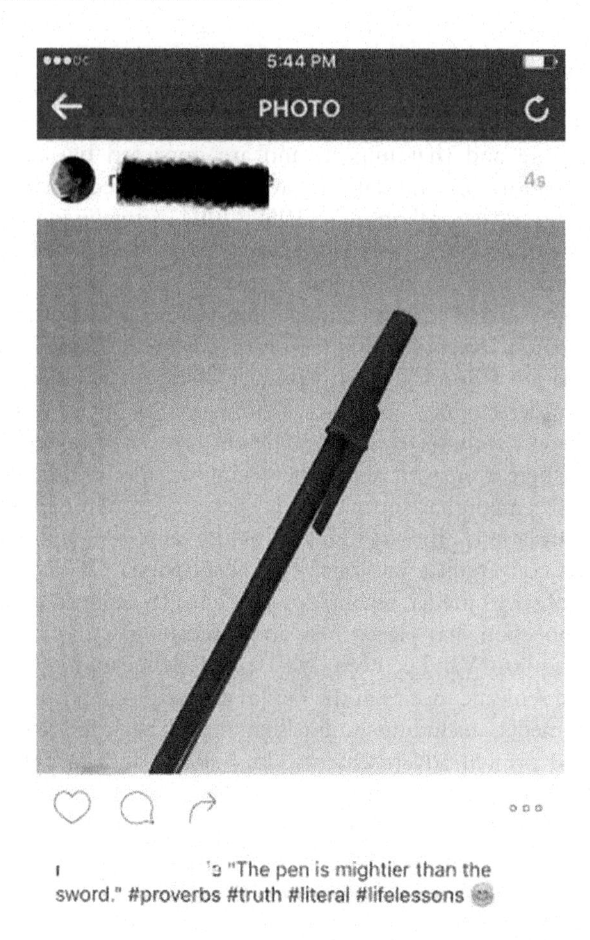

Fig. 3.1 Example of Instagram UGC including the user's uploaded photo and caption

linguistic signs or words (e.g. French, English or any other platform-supported natural language), or *Emoji* (an iconographic language comprising small images[10] that are, in a sense, comparable to, and perhaps a more modern version of, Egyptian hieroglyphics[11]), or using a mix of both natural languages and *Emoji*. Captions also generally include *hashtags*, which are words that are preceded by the hashtag symbol

(#) and which serve to index content according to specific topics (e.g. #translation would index the post alongside all other posts using the same hashtag[12]; in Fig. 3.1, the hashtags are #proverbs; #truth; #literal; #lifelessons).

Let us now suppose this UGC post required translation because the user wanted to provide a bilingual rendition to engage their international followers.[13] Where would the translation begin? Surely most would answer that the translation process should begin with the linguistic text (i.e. the caption), but given that *Instagram* gives primacy to visual content, proceeding in this manner might lead to significant oversights. In Fig. 3.1, the user has used the hashtag '#literal', which in fact directly connects to the content in the photograph: a pen. As we shall see in greater detail, all the semiotic elements in the screenshot are interconnected and multimodal (iconographic/linguistic and even tactile if we consider that *Instagram* engages its users to tap, scroll and swipe through content). This example illustrates the limitations of translation when it is understood exclusively as *interlinguistic verbal translation*. The intersemiotic and multimodal nature of UGC on platforms, such as *Instagram*, underscores the necessity for definitions of translation that allow translators to consider 'semiotic events' as a whole. But this of course has implications for translator training and education, a theme that will be discussed more exhaustively in Chap. 4.

Perhaps more radically, this type of UGC requires a new form of bilingualism. Costales (2011) asserts that English is currently the international *lingua franca*, that is an established natural language serving as a bridge language that makes communication possible between speakers who do not share the same native tongue. However, English might soon find itself threatened by a new *lingua franca*, the 'language' of *Emoji*, a 'picture-based language' that is being used at a noteworthy rate (Bangor University report 2015). This 'change of the linguistic guard' would confirm Ostler's (2010) hypothesis, which suggests that the dominant influence of English will progressively fade because of the impact of technology.[14] The statistics in the case of *Emoji* are worthy of attention: a study led by TalkTalk Mobile (Caddy n.d.; Doble 2015; Jones 2015), the first in-depth study of its kind in the United Kingdom, reveals that 62 % of respondents are using *Emoji* more than they were a year ago, with four in ten participants claiming to have sent messages exclusively in *Emoji*, that is to say *without the use of a verbal human language*. Moreover, the study cites that 72 % of younger participants (the 18–25 bracket) 'now find it easier to express their emotions with the pictorial symbols more than with words, with over half (51 %) believing Emoji have improved our ability to interact' (Bangor University 2015, online). In other words, the smiley face symbol at the end of the caption in Fig. 3.1 is felt to 'communicate' just as much, if not more than the words themselves. There is no doubt that in their social media UGC, advertisers, celebrities, politicians and other users looking to communicate and to sell their products to younger generations are turning to *Emoji* to relay their messages. And if the rise of *Emoji* continues in the way that the Bangor University report suggests, translators will now have to consider *Emoji* as a legitimate language to translate into and out of in situations where *Emoji* may not be acceptable or appropriate (e.g. *Emoji* functions perfectly within the context of OSM, but couldn't function, say, in a radio spot advertising the same product or service). In addition, even within the context of OSM, if we define translation as an intersemiotic transfer as per Jakobson's (1959/2004) classification, then there is a degree of translation that must occur between the picture, the caption and the selected *Emoji*.

That said, some might consider *Emoji* a 'post-translation' language given that the symbols that comprise it are thought to be 'almost universally recognisable' (Bangor University 2015, online), yet more evidence and research on the universality of this 'language' is required (its use is still a very recent phenomenon) to support or counter this assertion. Interestingly, in a short essay focusing on the history of punctuation, Vandendorpe (1999, 2009) discusses the use of emoticons, *Emoji's* precursor, and asserts the unlikelihood of these symbols replacing verbal expressions. He states (*ibid.*, p. 104):

> [...] emoticons belong to another code and represent a far-reaching attempt that transcends languages, an attempt to incorporate an iconic dimension into the written code. It is doubtful the graft will take, because these signs encounter significant resistance based as much on the verbal roots of the language as on the traditions surrounding written culture. [...] This [...] incompatibility will likely condemn them [emoticons] to remaining a marginal feature of writing, suitable mainly for e-mail and chat and for private relationships among adolescents, like their distinctive sociolinguistic codes.

Throughout the book in which this essay is included, Vandendorpe offers prescient observations on the evolution of text, writing and reading (the original content was written in 1999, long before mobile texting, smart-phones and OSM were as pervasive as they are today). However, the position taken here differs from Vandendorpe's with respect to emoticons being reserved exclusively for personal communication: though it is true that emoticons largely remained in the arena of personal and casual communication and alongside verbal text, as a newer language, *Emoji* has come to be used *in place of* other languages *completely*, for instance in text messaging (Bangor University 2015), in *Instagram* and *Snapchat* users' content captioning, and even in global brands' advertising (Tesseras 2015). Thus, *Emoji* is a far more sophisticated version of its punctuation-based predecessor (notably due to the addition of colour and symbols that do not relate to human emotions or facial expressions), and its popularity across generational divides suggests that it has a higher likelihood of adoption and staying power. *Emoji* is an example of how OSM and new technology can foster the uptake of artificial languages.

However, inasmuch as *Emoji* is not systematically taught in schools (which might then lessen its appeal) and is still reserved mostly to privileged and economically developed demographics who can afford 'to converse' on the devices that support *Emoji* (not all devices and platforms do), the likelihood of *Emoji* superseding English as a global *lingua franca* is unlikely, despite some of the enthusiastic claims made by Evans (Bangor University 2015) – not impossible, but unlikely. But TS should take note: as studies continue to investigate translation flows and asymmetries between the exchanges of cultural capitals, it might be wise to consider the ground gained by *Emoji* and the rise of artificial languages created to respond to new technological advancements. Will *Emoji* one day be spoken of in the way that International English (Reeves 2002) is today? Will *Emoji* pose a threat to translation in that it will erase the need for translation altogether? Does *Emoji* more effectively represent a politically neutral 'language' than other natural languages? What links can be made between *Emoji* and other artificial languages such as Esperanto[15]?

Due to its simplicity and tongue-in-cheek nature, it is unlikely that *Emoji* would ever be used exclusively as a scientific or technical language, especially in documents that carry any sort of legal or political bearing, which is a significant point of contrast from Esperanto, for instance, which could be used for these types of texts.[16] Nonetheless, it is apparent that on OSM, *Emoji* is a language of choice among many OSM users on various social platforms (McHugh 2016), regardless of the user nationality, native language or the generation to which they belong. Therefore, inasmuch as new translators prepare for the digital marketplace or inasmuch as veteran translators seek to renew their skills, having a base knowledge of new artificially created OSM 'languages' will be paramount to staying current, but also to staying competitive.

The significant use of hashtags on OSM also requires pause for thought. The non-linear nature of the Web, which has been discussed by Pym (2011a) and Vandendorpe (1999, 2009), implies a new kind of reading and referencing, and, by extension, a different way of thinking about translation. Vandendorpe (*ibid.*, p. 1) summarizes these implications in his introductory chapter:

> Until the late seventies, it was still possible to believe that the effects of computers would be felt only in scientific and technical fields. Today it is clear that computers and the technology associated with them are revolutionizing the way in which our civilization creates, stores, and transmits knowledge. They will eventually transform the most valuable tool human beings have created to build knowledge and develop their image of themselves and the world: text. And since text exists only in relation to reading, changes in text will have repercussions for reading, just as changes in reading will necessarily lead to the development of other modes of textuality. We do not read hypertext the same way we read a novel, and browsing the Web is a different experience from a book or newspaper.

The Web and, more specifically, OSM UGC call for 'paradigmatic' reading: instead of reading from start to finish, left to right, top to bottom (a linear and traditional representation of how we read), readers of Web-based content tend to follow a T- or F-shaped reading pattern[17] (Nielsen 2006, 2008). They will scan the top of the page rapidly and move downwards, scrolling backwards or forwards, or even skipping to a new webpage if the content includes hypertext linking to other, sometimes related, content. In this sense, reading becomes, as Vandendorpe explains, akin to a 'spreading out' rather than a 'digging for' process. As readers move about the webpage, they can choose to click on hypertext that will then lead them to other associated content. Unlike reading a book, which in terms of time is usually a finite activity, Web 2.0 affords an infinite form of reading: one with no clear reading path or ending. Though online readers usually know where they start their reading, where they end is a different matter. Translators are also readers, first and foremost; so it stands to reason that if reading has changed, then how translators read and translate texts has as well.

If we return to Fig. 3.1, the verbal text included in the caption calls for paradigmatic reading. Setting aside the intersemiotic connections to be made with the picture in the post, the verbal caption includes the use of four hashtags. Similarly to hypertext, which can prompt readers to 'move' to another text by clicking the highlighted word, phrase, picture or link, hashtags can prompt users to jump to another page or another UGC post. However, hashtags are different from hypertext in that they serve to index UGC posts according to specific content topics. In other words, a hashtag has the potential to redirect a reader, but it also affords the possibility of seeing what other UGC posts are indexed under the same hashtag. Interestingly, posts can vary significantly in meaning and connotation, yet still be indexed under the same hashtag. For instance, in the case of Fig. 3.1, a user could click on '#truth' and be redirected to all the *Instagram* posts that also have used '#truth'. Unlike hypertext that usually connects the reader to related content (i.e. there is a direct connection to be made by the hypertext and the content being read, for instance, a link to a key term's definition, or a cited report as it often happens on *Wikipedia*), hashtags do not necessarily redirect to explicitly related content. For example, if we use Fig. 3.1, we may ask: what is the immediate connection between the depicted pen and #truth? Clicking on the hashtag 'truth' will not lead a user to better understand the photo of the pen: no definitions or sources or further reading would be prompted. This poses a significant theoretical challenge for the translation of hashtags: translating a hashtag is not just a matter of translating only the signifier or only the signified (or even the sign as a whole), it is a matter of understanding why specific hashtags are chosen over others and how they associate seemingly disparate UGC. Further, to translate a hashtag might mean to completely alter the indexing for the subsequent target reader. For instance, supposing '#truth' were to be translated into the French '#vérité', this would radically impact the indexing of the translated (TT) post. The hashtag '#truth' generates 31,111,952 posts on *Instagram*, whereas the French hashtag '#vérité' only generates 42,240 posts.[18] Further, the user posts generated by the English hashtag are not the same as those generated by the French hashtag. Translation, of course, demands transformation, whether on the level of signifiers or signifieds, as many translation theories have shown over the many turns of TS. However, transforming a hashtag – translating a hashtag – means embedding a post within an entirely different set of posts, which can have implications on a number of levels. In the case of corporate or sponsored *Instagram* content (i.e. posts that are created with the intent to advertise, to sell or to promote), indexing a post using a less popular hashtag could mean fewer views, which, in turn, could mean less engagement and fewer sales. Perhaps this is why many sponsored accounts choose to publish ST captions alongside their translations (i.e. ST and TT co-exist in a single post caption), or use hashtags sparingly to avoid the issue of indexing altogether. Searches on *Instagram* show that some individual accounts (i.e. that aren't sponsored or of an overt corporate nature) favour a captioning model in which the verbal part of the caption is in the user's native language (e.g. French, German and Polish) and the hashtags are almost always exclusively in English – which indicates that the use of hashtags might function as another instance of International English.

As of yet, there does not seem to be a single authoritative strategy for the translation of hashtags. In professional practice, there are different schools of thought. For instance, *Library and Archives Canada* chooses to translate hashtags used in their *tweets*, with research conducted by the social media team to ensure that the hashtags used in both languages resonate with both target audiences. *Library and Archives Canada*'s social media team has decided, in line with most Canadian federal government departments, to have separate accounts for English and French content. Effort is made to use target language hashtags that are equally engaging and that index with a baseline number of posts[19] (hashtags, ideally, should not only index one or two posts, as it is unlikely the topic in question is of popular interest). Figures 3.2 and 3.3 are examples of two *tweets* that have been translated (English into French), but presented on separate accounts. In the English versions, the hashtags #DYK (standing for 'did you know?') and #OTD (standing for 'on this day') are used so that *Twitter* readers who follow these tags can readily find the posts indexed to connect similar UGC. These acronyms are not commonly used among French speakers; thus, alternative hashtags had to be found in the French. In this particular example, we notice two different strategies. In the first set of *tweets*, in the French version of the '#DYK santa' post, the hashtag has been omitted altogether (strategy = omission). While the hashtag '#SaviezVous' is quite popular and could have performed the same function as '#DYK', it is likely that *Twitter*'s restricted character count did not allow the translator to include the longer French hashtag. However, because the hashtag '#hockey' is still used, and because '#hockey' is a hashtag that indexes significant post volume in both languages, little is lost. In the second set of

Fig. 3.2 Example of two tweets from Library and Archives Canada's Twitter account (English version)

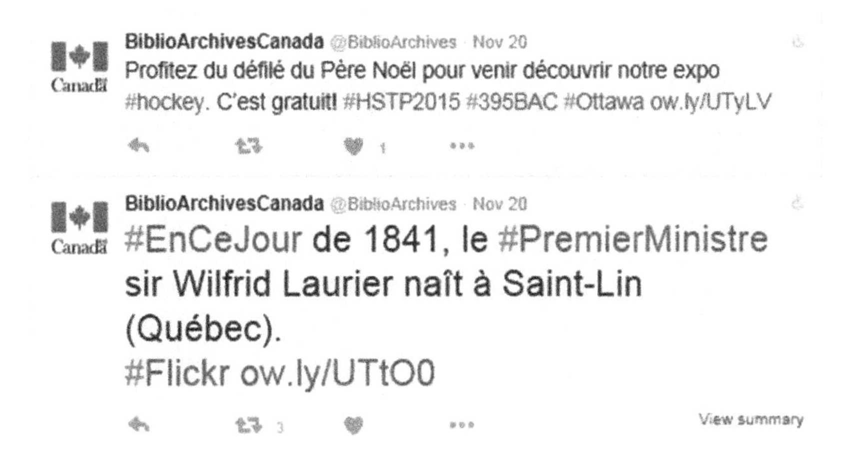

Fig. 3.3 Example of two tweets from Bibliothèque et Archives Canada's Twitter account (French version)

tweets, a second strategy is used: i.e. that of using a functionally equivalent hashtag. In this second example, '#OTD' has been translated by '#EnCeJour', the common French equivalent (i.e. both hashtags refer to the same conceptual reference, but each hashtag indexes differently). Although the hashtags in each *tweet* will direct users to different content, the content is still thematically similar – thus, the indexing is equally effective, or, in other words, functional (strategy = finding a hashtag in the target language that performs a similar thematic function).

Hashtags prompt a new way of thinking about equivalence. Though the debate on equivalence has never been exclusively a matter of formal equivalence (e.g. 1:1, word-for-word), hashtags underscore the necessity of understanding the paradigmatic nature of OSM content. To translate a hashtag effectively, one must consider indexing and topic popularity. Hashtags are effective and functional if they connect UGC to a larger constellation of posts; otherwise, the content becomes for the most part irrelevant. Translators who translate content similar to that shown in Figs. 3.2 and 3.3 must understand the connotations of the hashtags they use and must stay abreast of popular topics with higher rates of indexing in order to provide functional and effective solutions.[20] Therefore, bilingualism and biculturalism, argued to be the very foundation of translator competency, are clearly insufficient in the translation of OSM content.

Returning now to the discussion of the multimodal (i.e. different modes or media used to communicate signs) and multisemiotic (i.e. the different semiotic systems used in communication)[21] nature of OSM, another significant advancement brought forth by higher Internet speeds, mobile technology and photo-sharing OSM platforms is the possibility of uploading and sharing visual content effortlessly and at unprecedented speed. According to a piece in the *New York Times*, 'traditional' photography is on the decline, due to the rise of digital photography (Clifford 2010). Today, thanks to OSM platforms like *Facebook, Instagram, SnapChat, Pinterest, Flickr* and *YouTube*, which all enable photo-sharing and video-sharing to varying degrees, users can share, curate and view photos and videos with greater ease than previous generations of photographers, professional or amateur. As these types of hypervisual platforms proliferate, perhaps human communication is entering a new phase, one which is mediated far more significantly by visual content than the written word, which recalls Snell-Hornby's (2012, p. 370) reflection on the impact of technology on language: 'Modern global communication is instant and swift, visually forceful and linguistically fragmented.' This omnipresence of visual content recalls Régis Debray's concept of the 'videosphere' (1992). In his work, Debray posits three main eras of communication: the *logosphere*, the *graphosphere* and the *videosphere*. The *logosphere* marks an era in which primacy was given to the human sense of sound. During this period, the ear was seen to be superior to the eye – to hear something was more valid, in some cases, than seeing it (Vandendorpe 1999, 2009). When writing became more prevalent, this marked a shift towards what Debray calls the *graphosphere* – i.e. primacy of the written word. Today, given the hypervisual nature of many texts, particularly on the Web and on OSM platforms especially, there is no denying that sight has now become as important if not more important than sound and written text. Although multiple music-sharing OSM platforms exist (*Spotify* and *Soundcloud*, to name only two), none has managed to accrue the same number of users or to generate the same frequency of user visits as photo-sharing OSM platforms.[22] These data might suggest a contemporary preference among some users for visual content over auditory content, although it is important to note that video can include sound and many photos now include superimposed text (e.g. *memes*[23]) or are labelled with captions, as the previous *Instagram* example depicts in Fig. 3.1.

If indeed we are currently in the era of the *videosphere*, we might wonder how the rise of the visual impacts translation, and how it might continue to do so in the future. For one, the visual commands a different understanding of textuality, that is how does one 'read' images? Kress and Van Leeuwen (2006) as well as Baldry and Thibault (2005) have developed models to 'read' images that, although not originally designed to address social media content or UGC, can still be applied in such contexts. These models, however, are rather sophisticated and require complex analysis as well as detailed transcription. Nonetheless, these models can be extremely useful for translators and translation scholars looking to better understand and to elucidate the interplay between verbal text and visuals in their work (Desjardins 2013b). There have been arguments made elsewhere in favour of increased visual literacy (Rose 2007; Elkins 2008; Rose 2012) and, specifically, of training translators to be more 'visually literate', particularly in the area of audiovisual translation and advertising translation (Oittinen and Kaindl 2008). However, it is the instantaneous and prolific nature of visual content on social media that commands visual literacy more imperatively than ever before. If translators are seldom taught to think about translation beyond the verbal during their training, and if the translation industry continues to espouse a limited view of translation as well,[24] it is easy to see with the onslaught of visual OSM content how this position is not only myopic – especially since the plea for recognizing different types of translation significantly predates the contemporary 'OSM *videosphere*', for instance with the work of Jakobson (1959/2004) – but also how such a position could potentially signal the demise of part of the translation industry. Said differently, as an increasing number of companies and organizations, both for-profit and non-profit, and regardless of size, migrate to OSM platforms for most, if not all, of their corporate or organizational communication (i.e. liaising with stakeholders; customer Q&A; customer engagement; advertising; etc.), and as 'simplified' localization strategies seem to be shifting from primarily verbal content to increasingly visual content on OSM (e.g. *YouTube* tutorials featuring no verbal content whatsoever that recall the non-verbal *Ikea* instructions; *Instagram* posts featuring exclusively visual content, for instance, a picture of a new product captioned only by an *Emoji* representing a 'thumbs up'), the need for translation altogether perhaps becomes questionable, if not obsolete, that is, unless we reposition translation activity to fit these new realities.

The fact that translation is seen as a linguistic operation is arbitrary and based on a recursive normative system that continues to give precedence to interlingual/interlinguistic translation (Desjardins 2013b). For instance, in Canada, a system of norms defines what constitutes translation: legal norms (i.e. the *Official Languages Act*), institutional norms (government agencies; university translation programs) and administrative norms (cf. Toury 1978, 1980, 1995). Because the Canadian *Official Languages Act* supersedes any other language policy in the country, the federal and provincial public sectors must comply with this law. As a result, translation activity must follow this legal normative framework; therefore, not only is translation viewed primarily and exclusively as interlinguistic work, but primacy is given to two languages more specifically (English and French) over all others. While this is problematic on a number of levels (e.g. the symbolic superiority given to English and French which largely discounts languages of immigration and First Nations and Aboriginal languages; the legal 'exaltation' of English and French which also supposes cultural exaltations for those in power [Thobani 2007]), the focus on these two languages also professionally constrains translators, who often have expertise beyond mastery of purely verbal communication, as Gouadec (2007) indicates in his work on expected and required translator competencies in the marketplace of nearly a decade ago. The argument is then that yes, translation as it is sometimes defined, particularly in Canada, is undoubtedly threatened by the OSM *videosphere* and the new 'languages' of OSM (e.g. *Emoji*), but that is only if translation continues to be defined so narrowly. If translator training (institutional norm) and discourse on translation within TS (institutional norm) and the language industry (professional norm) were to increasingly include intersemiotic and intercultural competencies more explicitly, professional practice could lead to new avenues. This topic will be revisited in the discussion on translation training and professional practice.

3.5 Translation and the 'Like' Economy

In 2014, the American television station *PBS* aired a documentary titled *Generation Like* which examined the relationship between youth and social media. The documentary argued that what may seem like positive participatory culture[25] and empowerment through social media is in fact an insidious form of marketing, one that could be viewed as an exploitative form of youth engagement. In one example, we are introduced to 25-year-old Tyler Oakley, a young 'YouTuber' who readily promotes various products through his popular *YouTube* channel without necessarily receiving financial recompense, and who is increasingly lauded as a 'prosumer'[26] guru, one capable of showing major corporations how to better promote their products through youth and their social networks. When asked whether Oakley viewed his position as problematic (i.e. as exploitative), he didn't seem to think so. Leveraging the argument of community-building and collaboration associated with participatory culture, the young man suggested that his popularity in the social media sphere gave him the opportunity to help others in his network achieve similar fame and to obtain equal promotional perks. In another interview, Oakley stated that his social media fame has provided a platform for social issues he views as important, for instance, LGBT (lesbian, gay, bisexual and transgender) rights and suicide awareness (Grindley 2014). In other words, Oakley did not seem to mind trading 'likes' for new products and event tickets, nor did he seem to mind providing 'play labour' (Fuchs 2015)[27] (i.e. labour that extends beyond work hours and work wages) as this allowed him to also raise awareness for the causes he holds as important.

In a sense, Oakley's case recalls that of crowdsourcing. Many of those participating in OSM crowdsourced translation projects, for instance the translation of OSM platforms and community guidelines, are happy to do so due to the 'feel-good' factor of 'making the interface accessible around the world to people outside the community' (Dolmaya 2011, p. 102). They, like Oakley, view 'play labour' as a means of contributing to a cause they view as important (i.e. ensuring the content is accessible in a variety of languages). They, like Oakley, appreciate 'perks' in the forms of translator badges, translator profile photos, translator leaderboards or top contributor pages (*ibid.*). In short, they, like Oakley, do not seem to object to being remunerated in 'likes'. However, this is only a partial representation of the crowdsourced translation landscape.

In 2009, the professional social networking site *LinkedIn* surveyed their user base to assess the interest in platform translation (i.e. translation not only of the website infrastructure, but also of the mobile application). Translation work, the survey mentioned, would be remunerated symbolically, that is through non-monetary incentives, including some of the 'perks' mentioned previously (e.g. translator badges and 'free' premium accounts). Evidently, this caused division within the translation community. Of the 12,000 members polled, 50 % took offence to providing ostensibly 'free' translation for a for-profit commercial entity (*ibid.*) – data that suggests that professional translators, especially, viewed this crowdsourcing model as a means to undermine the value and worth of professional translation.[28] This event led to the creation of a *LinkedIn* group called *Translators Against Crowdsourcing by Commercial Businesses* (2015), which now lists 483 members. There is no denying the problems associated with crowdsourced translation, especially in the way of remuneration. However, as cases like Oakley's suggest, and given that the other 50 % of respondents in the *LinkedIn* 'crowdsourcing crisis' didn't seem to object to non-monetary remuneration, the time has come to consider how OSM might be changing how professional translation is remunerated.

Oakley's case (and he is not alone; other cases, particularly on *Instagram*, have shown how a strong OSM presence can lead to a meteoric rise in popularity, which usually translates into corporate sponsorships, free products and other 'benefits') demonstrates how some OSM users have come to accept different compensation models in lieu of more traditional forms of remuneration, such as salaries, in return for their 'play labour' hours. Some translators recognize that doing *pro bono* work for corporate entities can pay off in unexpected ways and boost their own business, which aligns with Posner's (2009) statements on how many *LinkedIn* professionals, not only translators, contribute 'free' expertise in return for recognition by other site members within the *LinkedIn* community. For a professional translator, especially, an increased social media presence via crowdsourcing can mean accruing more profile views from other members, which can drive new, and maybe longer-lasting, remunerated business.

More fundamentally, what we see in the Oakley and *LinkedIn* examples is a new type of social capital (Hanifan 1920) within OSM communities and a redefinition of symbolic capital (Bourdieu 1984, 1986) in light of the relationships and partnerships OSM affords – one that is embraced far more by Generation Y (also known as the 'Millennial Generation') than older generations using OSM. This is not to say that younger professional translators do not want to be paid in the same manner as their predecessors: studies do show that financial stability and proper remuneration are important to the millennial generation, but not at the expense of doing what they love (Shin 2014). They also want to use that symbolic capital as a potential source of new connections that should hopefully generate real income. Though more research on the matter is necessary, one hypothesis is that younger respondents and voluntary crowdsourcers engage in crowdsourcing because they are 'doing what they love' and find validation in forms of non-monetary compensation that can lead to interesting ventures prospectively. Does this undermine professional translation and the professional translation industry? Not necessarily; it does however mean a shifting landscape.

As McDonough Dolmaya (2011) argues, the crowdsourced translation of OSM platforms has given a new visibility to translators and translation. Whereas traditionally managed localization requires considerable human, financial and time resources, which can ultimately lead to the decision of *non-translation* (i.e. the decision *not* to localize or translate components of a website, application or platform), crowdsourcing makes the translation of large-scale initiatives, such as OSM platform translation, possible and therefore, by extension, visible. That said, McDonough Dolmaya indicates that languages with fewer online participants still remain at a disadvantage. Unlike French or Spanish – languages that have a large online community –'peripheral' languages (Heilbron and Sapiro 2007; Sapiro and Heilbron 2008; Fraisse 2013) do not have the same user base and therefore do not have the same resources from which to pool crowdsourcing participants. Though McDonough Dolmaya is correct in her assertion, and while there are problems with asymmetrical translation flows, the data isn't shocking: it replicates what occurs in the translation industry offline (UNESCO 2009; Brisset 2010). However, unlike professional 'offline' translation, the crowdsourcing model is not always dependent on accuracy, loyalty to an author, publishing house standards or market demands in quite the same way. This latitude, then, in fact proves to be beneficial to languages with fewer online users in that those who want social content and platforms translated can then essentially take matters into their own hands. Said differently, crowdsourcing gives users agency: the need for translation and the actual translation of content is no longer contingent on the decision-making power of corporations and organizations alone. Thus, while there is no denying that corporations have power and are involved in OSM platform translation, not to mention the implicit and explicit exploitation of 'play labour', we should be mindful that OSM users do have some unprecedented agency in determining what gets translated, what doesn't and how. This view, then, offers a necessary counterpoint to some of the criticism associated with 'play labour', which is valid, but does not seem to acknowledge the awareness and agency that many crowdsourcers and users of OSM platforms have. Among others,[29] Fuchs (2014, 2015) has taken an especially critical stance on this type of 'play labour' and the capitalist framework that underpins much of social media prosumerism. Using a predominantly Marxist approach, Fuchs (2015, p. 116) argues:

1. Social media play a role in the acceleration of the economy, politics and culture.
2. The emergence of crowdsourcing, play labour and presumption extends the working day to leisure time. This absolute surplus-value production is complemented by relative surplus-value production, in which more advertisements and more targeted ads are presented at the same time by making use of personalized advertising and economic surveillance.
3. Social media are an expression of the circumstance that the factory and the worker have become social and diffused into all realms of society. Exploitation has in capitalism always been extended into the household in the form of reproductive labour. Digital labour on social media means that yet more time that is spent outside of paid work conducted in factories and offices is becoming exploited. The amount and the intensity of the exploitation of unpaid labour have increased.
4. Targeted online advertising tries to make users consume more commodities by presenting ads to them.
5. Corporate social media are based on fictitious capital investments that hope that targeted advertising will result in high future profits. The actual success rate of targeted advertising in making users buy more commodities is, however, unknown, which makes social media highly prone to financial crisis.

There is no denying the astute and complex analysis involved in Fuchs' work, and the problems that arise when big corporations profit from ostensibly free labour. However, what Fuchs and others do not readily address is the fact that some, like Oakley, are not only *aware* of how they are being 'exploited', but they *do not mind it* and, in fact, find ways to leverage non-monetary remuneration to their advantage. In his documentary interview, Oakley frames the relationship he has with corporate entities almost as one of bartering. For some OSM users, then, an economy that runs on 'likes' is simply the new norm, and social media recognition is an ultimate form of exaltation.

Though Oakley is not a translator, his use of social media has shown a sort of subversion of power, a model that could prove applicable in the translation industry. There is no denying that corporations do indeed benefit from having Oakley advertise their products to a legion of faithful followers. But as the *PBS* documentary shows, Oakley now consults with corporate brands to show how mutually beneficial partnerships can be created. For instance, discontinued products that Oakley and his followers want to see restocked can be returned to the shelves now that Oakley and his followers have shown that a potential market still exists for the product in question. Of course, this does mean profit for the company, but the 'crowd' is also satisfied in having their request granted. The 'crowd' is, thanks to OSM and UGC, now able to negotiate terms on more symmetrical grounds.

However, another issue, specifically in the case of crowdsourced translation, is that of credentials and expertise. The crowdsourcing model means, essentially, that anyone who is willing to translate can translate (Bogucki 2009), regardless of training or experience. Translation, therefore, is more generally seen as a *skill* or *ability*, rather than a profession that requires training (García 2010). It is this belief that has led to the relative success (i.e. popularity and increased rates) of crowdsourced translation. Of course, this is disheartening and worrisome for any professional translator having invested considerable time, effort and financial resources to obtain their credentialing, be it through certification programs, professional workshops or university degrees. Some professional and credentialed translators are quick to assert that those without formal training lack competency, though many anecdotal examples exist to weaken this claim. So what are competent and professional translators to do in a context that enables anyone to be a translator[30]? Like Oakley, professional translators – those who have insight into translation theories, intercultural communication, translation technologies and translation quality assessment – ought, according to García (2010), to mobilize the value-added they can contribute to improve OSM translation *processes* (localization; crowdsourcing), rather than focusing exclusively on the threat posed by non-professional translators or the lack of quality in this type of language transfer. In other words, the OSM-savvy credentialed translator does not spend time worrying about those who are happy to contribute 'play labour' in the form of crowdsourced translation. They instead can consult with OSM platform programmers and developers as to how to improve the existing crowdsourced translation models (i.e. how to better assess quality; how to make crowdsourcing models more user friendly; how to integrate translation tools into the process; etc.). This line of thought runs parallel to the view expressed in an article featured in a thematic issue of the *Harvard Business Review* (2015), which focused on the 'man–machine collaboration'. In their article 'Beyond Automation', Davenport and Kirby (2015) propose strategies for sustaining employment in an age of 'very smart machines'. Although here the discussion is not about machine translation or translation memory, which pose another technological 'threat' that many professional translators worry about, OSM remains a form of (or application of) technology that could serve to overhaul existing translation processes. Further, as some OSM platforms integrate automatic machine translation into their social platforms (*Facebook,* for instance, has integrated *Microsoft's Bing Translation* [Fernandes 2011] to allow users to translate UGC), we see that crowdsourced translation is not the only 'threat' to professional and credentialed translators. Translators might want to consider OSM and integrated automatic machine translation as a technological advancement that could alter current professional practice significantly.

Davenport and Kirby (2015, p. 60) argue that many of the tasks carried out by professionals today will be automated in the near future. However, instead of viewing this as a problem, they propose viewing the situation in a different light:

> What if we were to reframe the situation? What if, rather than asking the traditional question – What tasks currently performed by humans will soon be done more cheaply and rapidly by machines? – we ask a new one: What new feats might people achieve if they had better thinking machines to assist them? Instead of seeing work as a zero-sum game with machines taking an ever greater share, we might see growing possibilities for employment. We could reframe the threat of *automation* [and even 'play labour'] as an opportunity for augmentation.

Davenport and Kirby's position is that professionals need to look at how current technological threats (they focus on automation and machines, but the argument could apply to Web 2.0 more generally) can in fact deepen work instead of diminishing it. Professional translators, those that have gone through extensive training, have a wealth of technical skills that can be used to inform the development of better technology and more effective/efficient crowdsourcing. However, it is also imperative that translators be OSM literate in order to perform this type of consultancy, which stresses the need to integrate social media competencies (and technological competencies beyond mastery of machine translation and computer-assisted translation tools more broadly) into translator training and education. If professional and credentialed translators wish to stay competitive in an increasingly crowdsourced and automated market, then traditional modes of training and thinking about translation need to adapt. Alternatively, for professional translators to stay a step ahead of the 'play labour' translator, it will be essential to find niches within the profession that wouldn't be economical or viable to automate or crowdsource.

A reframing of 'technology/crowdsourcing as opportunity' gives rise to a new form of translator agency. Translators who leverage their expertise in the form of Web 2.0 consultancy have a better likelihood of finding themselves at the heart of OSM platform *production*, or, metaphorically, in the position of being part of forethought, as opposed to being in a position of *reproduction*, or, afterthought.

In addition, it is not only professional translators that should view the current OSM landscape in more opportune terms. TS scholars can significantly contribute to industry-led studies seeking to better understand how OSM is used in different geographic locales. Singh et al. (2012, p. 686), for example, underscore that there is 'a lack of research into how companies can create truly global communities where participation is not hindered by language use'. In their work, these authors analyse global online user language preferences, including translation trends. They use the data to show how companies might better connect communities through 'linguistic integration' (*ibid.*). Interestingly, none of the three authors who conducted this research were TS researchers or professional translators. This is not to say that Singh et al.'s (*ibid.*) work has any less value; in fact, it is remarkable that translation would be given such 'visibility' in what is ostensibly a research piece on global marketing and global use of social media. However, additional layers of analysis could be added from a TS perspective. For instance, the authors propose using a custom real-time translation tool by the name of *GeoFluent* (which includes a cloud-based workflow/translation platform and translation memory capability – *Translation Workspace* – and machine translation) for the translation of OSM and UGC, but do not compare it with any other competing platforms such as *SDL Trados, WordBee, FlipLingo* and others. *GeoFluent* is a tool developed by the global company Lionbridge and it should be noted that Bostick, one of the article's co-authors, is a Lionbridge employee. It is also acknowledged that Lionbridge Technologies Inc. did help with data collection and presentation of the case scenarios included in the research. Thus, the impartiality regarding *GeoFluent*'s assessment in this particular analysis can be questioned. TS scholars who specialize in the study of translation technologies could conduct further research and provide additional insight as to which translation platforms perform best. After all, it is one thing for marketers to propose tools, but it is another when translation professionals and researchers can assess the value-added and performance of these tools themselves.

Moreover, while crowdsourcing models and cloud-based platforms can assist in what has been referred to as 'linguistic integration' to varying degrees, fundamental questions and critical questions – such as what happens when the idea of 'language' and 'text' are taking unprecedented forms in an era marked by hypervisual UGC – point to the insight TS research and professional translators can contribute. There is no denying that the translation industry is undergoing a seismic shift due to OSM and new communication technologies; however, this does not need to signify the end of the professional translator. Translators need, in the terminology of Davenport and Kirby (2015), to 'augment' their position – just as Oakley claims to have done so to great success.

3.6 Conclusion

This chapter has addressed some of technological changes that have impacted human communication. More specifically, consideration was given as to how Web 2.0 and OSM have modified communicational behaviours in more recent years. Because translation is a form of communication, it follows that these behavioural shifts also impact, to varying degrees, translation, be it in the way that translation is conceptualized, defined, practised and recognized. It is apparent that OSM have impacted how texts are read: there is no way to read a UGC post in a linear manner, especially given the paradigmatic nature of hashtag indexing and the multimodal make-up of most UGC content. Further, mobile technology and OSM have given rise to a new artificial language, *Emoji*, that poses many questions for translation, notably that of whether or not translation is still relevant when a visual language that purports to universality exists. In addition, intersemiotic translation can no longer be seen as a distant cousin to interlinguistic translation; in an era saturated by images – to recall Debray's *videosphere* – it is probable that visual literacy will become of equal importance as verbal literacy Translators – particularly those working in multimedia or predominantly web-based environments – should therefore be prepared. Finally, the crowdsourcing of OSM platforms, such as *LinkedIn*, has come under scrutiny for the role it plays in undermining the professional translation industry, translator remuneration and the professional translator's status. However, this threat can be relativized and we should not be so quick to assume ignorance in those that engage in 'play labour'. A translator's social capital and symbolic capital can increase if they play the OSM game to their advantage: that is the power of augmentation at a time when corporations rely on the crowd to generate profits.

The next chapter will focus on three ways translator training can adapt to the new realities and demands generated by OSM and Web 2.0.

Notes

1. Research following a similar thesis has been pursued by Sumner et al. (2012, p. 386) that connects the anti-social traits of 'the Dark Triad' (narcissism, Machiavellian tendencies, and psychopathy) and individual activity on *Twitter* using linguistic analysis.
2. While there is a tendency to believe that OSM is becoming the primary gateway for accessing news, a collection of studies surveyed by Wihbey (2014) suggests this is not the case. The Internet, more broadly, does constitute one of the ways people access and consume news, but usually readers go directly to news sites, as opposed to obtaining their news exclusively through OSM. OSM, however, is viewed as an 'important tool' for 'discovering' news (*ibid.*), meaning that users are likely to come across a topic of interest via OSM, but then go directly to the source for more information. Yet, as demographics change, especially with the millennial generation that tends to comprise a far greater number of 'digital natives' (Prensky 2001, p. 1), and with the rates for mobile device ownership

increasing, this may accelerate the shift towards a more diversified news ecosystem, in which OSM are a dominant news source (Wihbey 2014).

3. That translation can 'skew' information is not a novel idea. Theo Hermans' (1985) seminal publication *The Manipulation of Literature* is perhaps one of the most important references on the topic in the field of TS. However, the distinction that should be underscored here has to do with the medium: OSM and digital technologies can disseminate information at unprecedented speed, whereas in the context of translated literature, the process of dissemination and the speed of dissemination are quite different.
4. In an email interview, Clay Shirky (Wihbey 2014, p. 12) an associate professor of journalism at NYU, explains to Wihbey: 'People who are clicking on links on social media are in a social context, whereas people who go directly to a news sites have in mind something more solitary and focused.'
5. A recent article in *The Guardian* (Burke 2016) discusses in greater detail how terrorists are leveraging digital media to keep the public's attention. Translation is not explicitly mentioned, but it is rather doubtful that foreign terrorist cells and intelligence agencies are not conducting translation activity online to some degree. Therefore, future research in this area is warranted.
6. Technopedia (2016a, online) defines social media monitoring as 'a process of using social media channels to track, gather and mine the information and data of certain individuals or groups, usually companies or organizations, to assess their reputation and discern how they are perceived online. Social media monitoring [SMM] is also known as social media listening and social media measurement'.
7. 'Social media monitoring is the active monitoring of social media channels for information about a company or organisation. Several different providers have created tools to facilitate the monitoring of a variety of social media channels from blogging to internet video to internet forums. This allows companies to track what consumers are saying about their brands and actions. Companies can then react to these conversations and interact with consumers through social media platforms' (*Financial Times* 2016).
8. While the definition of languages for special purposes has usually incorporated non-verbal elements, the view taken here is one that coincides with normative definitions of translation in the Canadian public sector (cf. Desjardins 2008, 2013b).
9. Due to copyright and privacy, using fictional content was deemed more appropriate.
10. *Emoji* is the progression of previously used *Emoticons* (facial expressions conveyed using punctuation symbols such as the comma, the period and parentheses [cf. Dresner and Herring 2010]). While *Emoji* today largely comprises visual iconography related to human facial expressions, the

language now includes a variety of other images. In an announcement made by the Unicode Consortium in 2015, 38 additional Emoji had been accepted as candidates for Unicode 9.0, some of which – for instance Mother Christmas and a carrot – have nothing to do with human facial expressions or basic human emotions (Davis 2015). This suggests that *Emoji* is evolving to be a more complex language that accounts for objects, activities and abstract icons (e.g. dots or lines) and extends beyond human facial expressions.

11. This is a claim made by Professor Vyv Evans (Bangor University), whose work has been reported by the *BBC* (Doble 2015) and *The Guardian* (Jones 2015).
12. 'Hashtags are an emergent convention for labelling the topic of a micro-post [UGC] and a form of metadata incorporated into posts' (Zappavigna 2012, p.1).
13. A 'follower' on *Instagram* and on *Twitter* is a user who has chosen to subscribe to receive updates about another user's UGC. This is akin to *Facebook's* 'friends'.
14. It should be noted, however, that Ostler does not maintain that English would be replaced by a new *lingua franca* per se.
15. Esperanto is a constructed or artificial language that was created in the late nineteenth century. Since its creation, its number of speakers has risen. Technology has also played a role in its uptake: the popular language application *DuoLingo* now offers Esperanto learning modules (DuoLingo 2015) and *Google Translate* added the language to its list in 2012 (Buckley 2012).
16. Fettes (2005) suggests that scientific writing in Esperanto flourished after the First World War.
17. The 'T' and 'F' shapes represent the direction followed by the viewer's eyes (i.e. 'eyeflow').
18. The number of posts indexed under these hashtags is based on data retrieved on 27 December 2015.
19. This baseline number is usually determined by the communications or marketing team; therefore, the baseline can vary widely.
20. It should be noted that effectiveness can be a quantifiable metric: user engagement can be measured on the basis of interaction, for instance, in the case of *Twitter*, the number of *retweets* or *likes* a post generates among *followers*. Thus, *Twitter* translation is effective when both the source and target tweet generate similar engagement.
21. The distinction between these terms was further explored in Desjardins (2008, 2013b).
22. According to a report published by TechCrunch (Dillet 2013), *Soundcloud* had 250 million active listeners/users, whereas *Statista* (2016) indicates *Instagram* now has over 400 million active users.

23. According to the Merriam-Webster dictionary (Meme 2016), a *meme* is an 'idea, behavior, style or usage that spreads from person to person within a culture'. In social media 'culture', a *meme* usually refers to content that has gone viral, and many OSM *memes* now comprise a photo superimposed with bold, white text, sometimes including intentionally misspelled words, references to different social media subcultures or references to pop culture items (Technopedia 2016c, online).
24. This may not be the case on an international scale; however, in Canada, given the direct association between translation and official languages policy, most translation schools in the country train students in the two official languages exclusively. Further, job postings for translator positions rarely require translators to be proficient in languages that are not verbal in nature. These two examples point to the fact that implicitly, precedence is given to the verbal over the visual.
25. Jenkins (2008, p. 331) defines participatory culture as culture 'in which fans and other consumers are invited to actively participate in the creation and circulation of free content' and lists civic engagement, collaboration, mentorship, belief in making a difference and social connection as some of the defining characteristics of this culture.
26. The term 'prosumer' was coined by Toffler (1980) to refer to consumers that are at once producers and consumers of cultural products. It is widely used in media and social media studies in relation to OSM UGC.
27. 'All hours spent online by users of Facebook, Google and other comparable social media constitute work time, in which data commodities are generated, and potential time for profit realisation' (Fuchs 2015, p. 112).
28. 'Many professional translators (who represented about 50% of the 12,000 survey respondents) took offence to being asked to volunteer to translate for a commercial organization' (Dolmaya 2011).
29. Cf. Terranova (2004), Van Dijck and Nieborg (2009) and Costales (2011).
30. The Web, because of its ease of access, might make it easier for a layperson to contribute to a crowdsourced translation project. The question of credentialing is also relevant offline, as the term 'translator' is not a protected title in the majority of regions and countries. However, offline, there is a higher likelihood that employers would at least screen for some form of experience or credentialing, whereas this is less the case online.

CHAPTER 4

Translation and Social Media: In Training

Abstract This fourth chapter examines how current translator training and education are not sufficiently addressing key competencies needed for the digital age, with specific focus given to competencies associated with online social media (OSM) and translation programmes within Canadian universities. While no translation programme can address every aspect of professional translation, this chapter argues in favour of integrating OSM literacy and competencies within the translation curriculum. Strategies that might be helpful to those teaching undergraduate translation courses or for those trying to fine-tune their own skills are proposed throughout the chapter. These strategies might also provide inspiration for other translation-related curriculum development. A case is made for using social media in the classroom to foster participatory culture(s), as well as for exposing students to social media monitoring (SMM). The underlying argument is that if translator trainees are not taught OSM competencies, they will not be able to compete with elite bilinguals with more 'attractive' disciplinary profiles, be it elite bilinguals with computer programming, web design or communications backgrounds.

Keywords Translator training · Competencies · Digital age · Translation programme · Professional translation · Translation · Curriculum · Undergraduate · Curriculum development · Participatory culture · Social media monitoring

R. Desjardins, *Translation and Social Media*, Palgrave Studies in Translating and Interpreting, DOI 10.1057/978-1-137-52255-9_4

4.1 Introduction

In recent years, the debate surrounding the role that university education should play in preparing undergraduates and post-graduates for the workplace has been contentious, especially across North American campuses. Henry A. Giroux (2007, p. 7), for instance, addresses what he refers to as the 'military-industrial-academic complex' – a term he borrows from the US Senator William Fulbright[1] – that affects many North American campuses and that trains students to be nothing more than consumers, workers and soldiers. Giroux's position is not that corporations should not have a role in higher education, but rather, that their influence and wealth be used in ways that promote increased democratic public life, public welfare and critical thought (Jaschik 2007). In other words, Giroux does not believe that education should be fashioned solely in relation to, or in response to, the business world and the military. This position is commendable; however, it poses some significant challenges for the undergraduate and post-graduate training of translators, as this chapter will reveal. Translation, unlike other language-focused or arts-focused disciplines, is a practice-based profession that *subsequently* paved the way for the birth of an academic discipline, i.e. translation studies. Thus, those who choose to study translation, particularly at the undergraduate level, may have a different rationale than students coming into other disciplines in the arts and the humanities. In a related manner, most aspiring translators must graduate from a recognized translation programme in order to find viable employment and to obtain professional accreditation. In this sense, translator training obtained through a vetted university programme or course must therefore include vocational teaching components that are in direct response to the industry, even if, as Giroux suggests, the university's mission should not be to train 'workers'. An argument could then be made that vocational training that speaks exclusively to corporate or industry motives should be obtained via other modes of instruction outside of university campuses. Translation, for instance, could be 'taught' through workshops or professional development seminars. However, as it stands, translation is taught, most often, in universities. This raises an important point, which is that when we speak of 'training translators', it is important to specify the context in which the training is taking place, as training contexts have different purposes and may address different aspects of a field or discipline. The professional workshop does not necessarily address the same training objectives as the undergraduate degree in the arts or humanities (the faculties in which translation studies [TS] or translation programmes are usually subsumed). However, while

Giroux's position appears to be that university training should disassociate itself from corporate ties, the fact remains that *students* may not agree with this position: they want their undergraduate and graduate training to reflect market realities – they want to know how to be employable 'workers', and this seems to be the case especially in undergraduate translator trainees in particular.

In related debates on the subjects of training and translation, others have focused on translator training strategies more specifically (Kiraly 1995; Kelly 2005) and have addressed the different needs and expectations of translation trainees. In this chapter, specific consideration will be given to translator training within the context of undergraduate education. On-going professional development (or continuing professional development) and professional workshops do contribute significantly to improving translator expertise and competencies,[2] but the context in which these workshops are offered varies greatly from the context in which undergraduate university training takes place. The same can also be said of the expected outcomes from each of these types of training. On the one hand, the professional workshop might be meant to introduce one particular piece of software to a professional in-house translation team (i.e. to introduce a fixed and singular objective), whereas on the other hand, translation taught in the context of undergraduate training has a much larger horizon of expected outcomes, from professional aptitude to general critical thinking.

While the position taken here is one that largely agrees with Giroux's (i.e. that trainees should not be trained exclusively within the 'military-industrial-academic' paradigm), there is no denying that training translators requires trainers, educators and professors to teach to market demands, just as the same can be said of any profession or vocation, from health care provision (doctors, nurses, emergency service providers) to the practice of law. If undergraduate translation training were to consist exclusively of the critical study of translation (something akin to comparative literature or English literature, for instance), rather than in imparting very pragmatic competencies to answer to market realities, such as the ability to use machine translation (MT) efficiently or the ability to draft a legally admissible freelance contract, then it is likely that new graduates entering the marketplace would do so without fundamental and necessary skills. Therefore, without ignoring the importance of critical thought and intellectual autonomy, or some of the constraints and challenges associated with curriculum development (e.g. university bureaucracy keeping pace with the market; centralization; international student cohorts; budget restrictions; cost of upgrading technology), this chapter focuses more specifically on training avenues that are in line with what prospective employers are seeking from university graduates in translation, with particular attention given to gaps identified in Canadian translator training. The implication is that teaching 'to the translation market' does not mean training translators who are unable to think critically. Nor does it mean training translators *only* to be workers. On the contrary, exposing trainees to professional case studies, as well as to tools and technology that are pervasive in the marketplace (which includes for-profit, non-profit and governmental sectors), can afford many opportunities for the discussion of ethics, democracy, citizen engagement and unequal distributions of power. As studies continue to indicate relationships between entrepreneurship and innovation, universities will have to consider ways of integrating entrepreneurial and experiential content into the curriculum (Chiose 2016). For translator training, this might mean integrating new modules that address entrepreneurial competencies, so that within the translation curriculum, such skills are further developed. As Judith Cone (cited in Chiose 2016: online), the vice-chancellor of commercialization at the University of North Carolina, explains: 'If we don't include an entrepreneurial mindset in university education, we are missing the boat. [. . .] We feel that we want all students to understand the world they're going into. It's a different economy that is very dependent on the startup [entrepreneurial] sector.' Her position echoes that of Vogel (2015, pp. 106–107), who has written on the youth unemployment crisis. He states:

> When we think about a 21st century education system we must envisage a system that addresses the mismatch between what is being taught in our schools and the skills, knowledge, and experiences demanded by the current labor market. We must ask ourselves what the curriculum of tomorrow might look like, what skills are most important for our students, and which methodologies and resources will best transmit these new themes and skills to our young people; and ultimately how schools and universities can best prepare students for the workplace. [. . .] There need to be major changes to both how we teach and, in particular, what we teach. [. . .] Today, employers are arguing that students need to demonstrate that they have acquired applied knowledge within their field, which would better prove they could aptly perform in the workplace. [. . .] This signifies that labor market requirements are demanding a shift in classroom instruction.

Indeed, the current North American economy is grim for many prospective employees and recent graduates. Notably, the Bank of Canada recently predicted a 'gloomy 12-month employment outlook', adding that 'hiring intentions are weaker for most sectors in most regions' (Galt 2015, online). However, despite this less than ideal employment outlook, Shari Angle, vice-president of special projects for the recruitment firm *Adecco*, reports that the market is increasingly 'looking to recruit bilingual candidates across a wide spectrum of occupations' and that 'increasingly, candidates for executive positions are expected to have social media skills' (cited in Galt 2015, online).

Angle's comments are significant for translators and translators-in-training: if translators, who by definition must be bilingual as a base requirement, have social media skills, then they are well positioned for employment despite the employment forecast. At a minimum, then, social media literacy and competencies should be integrated into translator training.

A recent survey of Canadian translation undergraduate programmes and curricula conducted for this book shows that of the eight Canadian universities that offer a B.A. (undergraduate) degree in translation, none offer a course (or module) focusing exclusively on online social media (OSM) and translation.[3] And though some programmes do offer courses on Web translation and localization, the official course descriptions do not account for any OSM or user-generated content (UGC) explicitly. This survey thus reveals two crucial shortcomings in terms of translator training in the digital era, at least in Canada.

The first problem is that courses in localization are not offered in every Canadian translation programme, meaning that depending on where students are trained, they may in fact never have exposure to localization and localization tools by the time they graduate – a significant issue given the need and demand for localized websites (Pym 2011b). As Pym remarks (*ibid.*, p. 420): 'Few trainee translators acquire the multimedia and interactive skills most in demand at the more creative points of the industry, and those who do acquire such skills are unlikely to seek long-term employment doing nothing but decontextualized string replacement.' The data therefore suggests that translation training is inconsistent across Canadian universities, which, although unsurprising given the autonomy involved in curriculum design, is problematic for student employment and professional accreditation. In other words, students who have had exposure to localization and web-based tools will have better employment odds, or at least a larger range of employment options to choose from, than those who have never had the opportunity within their training programme to be exposed to this content. As a result, this creates an asymmetry between Canadian translation graduates on a national scale.

A second shortcoming in Canadian undergraduate translation curricula, which is equally if not more significant, is that of the lack of OSM training. OSM skills are paramount in today's workplace and the use of OSM is becoming increasingly inescapable, regardless of job title, as Angle notes (cf. Galt 2015). This fact alone makes a solid case for inclusion of OSM literacy and competencies within translator training. Of course, no single undergraduate programme can address all the skills and competencies required for the marketplace, but because of the increasing presence and use of OSM in human communication, and because translation is an important means to ensure cross-cultural communication, it follows that translator training should consider OSM as part of the contemporary curriculum.

An argument could be made that translation training that increasingly focuses on OSM and other Web 2.0 technologies dilutes language-focused content and opens the doors for more and more translation trainees to migrate to other fields once they graduate. For instance, instead of becoming translators, these graduates might choose to be OSM content managers or curators instead. However, this should not be seen as inherently problematic. Many prominent voices in translation, from TS scholars to trainers to professional translators, have argued and shown the intrinsic multidisciplinarity and interdisciplinarity of translation (Snell-Hornby 1988; Snell-Hornby et al. 1994; Lambert 1997/2006, 2012; Gambier 2014). So why would it not be a good thing, as a logical outcome of multidisciplinary, interdisciplinary and even transdisciplinary training, to see students obtain employment in which translation might not necessarily be the core task, but for which translation insights are invaluable? There is a degree of disconnect between the call for more interdisciplinarity at the level of research discourse in TS and what appears in some training contexts. The survey of Canadian university translation curricula shows[4] that translation training at the undergraduate level focuses primarily on 'core' language-centric courses: comparative stylistics, legal/medical/specialized/technical/literary translation, grammar courses, introductory courses in translation technologies and translation theories. Only four of the eight Canadian universities with accredited translation programmes offer localization or 'web and multimedia' courses, some of which are in fact courses listed under a different disciplinary code, suggesting that these are courses taught in different departments altogether. Moreover, none of these courses seem to escape Canada's 'obstinate' institutional bilingualism (Gambier 2014), meaning that all core translation courses and Web/localization courses are taught within the framework of English↔French transfer, which, at a time of increased immigration, is incongruous with the actual demographic and linguistic make-up of the country (Desjardins 2013b). Of course to this we might add the issue of other semiotic languages (such as *Emoji*; see Chap. 3) which do not even register at all.

Further, the issue is not only one of *preparing* students for the marketplace, but also one of *reflecting* on the evolution of communication within translator training. Unfortunately, it appears that training is not always apace with job realities. Although Gouadec (2007) does a formidable job in describing the profession and what skills translators *need* to know in order to find good employ, this does not always find a counterpart in actual training, chiefly when it comes to technological competencies. Some progress has been made in the last 10 years since the publication of Gouadec's work – for instance, most Canadian universities now have online student forums and WiFi access – but some challenges regarding the integration of information and communication technologies still remain: labs are expensive; software licenses are expensive; and these constraints are even more pronounced on campuses with fewer resources. Technology itself, also, evolves rapidly, which means that financial limitations aren't the only explanation. These are all valid reasons. However, there is another hidden constraint, one that is seldom addressed because it is a contentious issue: the generational divide. Social media are the 'voice' of the Millennial Generation, the voice of those who are 'digital natives' (Prensky 2001, p. 2). The reality is that most who are in trainer, professor or lecturer positions, that is, those who are training the millennial generation of translators, are also 'digital immigrants' (*ibid.*, p. 3). Without intending ageism or gross overgeneralization, 2011 data from Statistics Canada (Service Canada 2015) show that university professors tend to fall into two main age brackets: 45–64 years, and 64 and over. While these data are specifically for the Quebec region (i.e. only one Canadian province), it is noted that these trends are more or less reflected in the rest of the country. As Prensky (2001, 2006, 2007) notes, the 'digital' fluency of this latter demographic cannot be the same as that of the Millennial Generation, who has never known a time without the Internet. Most undergraduate students are then more likely to be well-versed in OSM trends and Web 2.0 technologies compared to the professors who are training and teaching them (Stewart et al. 2010), particularly in fields where OSM is not a core part of the curriculum. To add to this reality, social media, especially outside of communications departments or media studies departments, were initially seen as a fad, a distraction (Bugeja 2007) and something unworthy of serious academic attention. More recently, some have underscored the implicit privilege of schools or universities who can 'afford' technology and tech-savvy experts, and those that cannot (see, for example, Selwyn 2011), either due to their geographic location (inability to attract top talent based on remote location), a lack of human resources (e.g. adequately trained staff and faculty) or limited financial resources. Despite these challenges, however, training programmes cannot continue to overlook OSM literacy.

Building on the concept of augmentation[5] as proposed by Davenport and Kirby (2015), this chapter aims to show some of the directions translator training could take in order to impart OSM and UGC competencies relevant to today's translation marketplace. Though not exhaustive, these directions can lead to additional research and training initiatives that might be beneficial for newer generations of translator trainees.

4.2 Addressing Multimodal and Multisemiotic Translator Training in Light of OSM

Social media literacy and social media skills constitute a whole area of study and training. It is impossible to imagine that translator trainees could be trained in social media competencies to the degree that students in media studies or communications might be. However, much like the other areas of expertise that are incorporated into translator training (e.g. medical terminology, localization, legal terminology, scientific and specialized translation), the belief here is that some elements that pertain to social media could be relatively easily integrated into existing translation courses or modules, be it in the context of specialized translation, in the discussion of translation theories or as case studies for research projects. In the four sub-sections that follow, four key specificities of OSM worthy of curriculum integration will be overviewed. These four specificities pertain to the moving target of social media audiences; tactile 'textuality'; hashtag indexing; and the importance of visual literacy. Again, the goal is not to train translators

051

P110904N8

ST HELENS COLLEGE

8

ISBN	Qty	Sales Order
9781137522542	1	F 21309368 1

Customer P/O No	Cust P/O List
SKB104/03	39.99 GBP

Title: Translation and social media : in theory, in training and in

Format: C (Cloth/HB)
Author: Desjardins, Renée
Publisher: Palgrave Macmillan
Fund:
Location: Library
Loan Type:
Coutts CN: 33451697

Order Specific Instructions

Ship To: UK 51909001 F
ST HELENS COLLEGE
THE LIBRARY
WATER STREET
ST HELENS
MERSEYSIDE
WA10 1PP

Volume:
Edition:
Year: 2017.
Pagination: 134 pages
Size: 21 cm

Routing *2
Sorting
Y01H11Z
Covering – BXAXX
Despatch
Available: EBSCO, ProQuest Ebook Central

PROQUEST LLC:

051483424 ukrwlg14 RC2

to comply exclusively with market demands, but to also ensure a critical reflection on how translation operates (or doesn't) in the context of social media activity.

4.2.1 Who Is the Target Audience?

As Chap. 3 sought to illustrate, OSM and UGC underscore how textuality and language can no longer be defined according to more 'traditional' conceptualizations. For instance, users' ability to update, edit or delete UGC at any given time on OSM platforms makes the very concept of one 'original' and definitive source text problematic. Moreover, foundational functionalist translation theories, such as *Skopostheorie* (for an overview of functionalist approaches, see Nord [1997]) which assert that translation activity should be conducted with the target audience and target purpose in mind, rest on shaky ground when, more than ever, 'targets' become increasingly difficult to pinpoint on social media. Said differently, the translation of OSM content can be problematized if audience and purpose are guiding principles. When individual users post a *Facebook* status update or *tweet* on *Twitter*, the exact target audience can never be wholly determined, especially when a user's profile or UGC is made public.[6] In the case of for-profit and non-profit entities, the same is also true: their UGC can reach virtually anyone as well, provided their settings are public (which is most often the case). And though many social platforms do allow a degree of analysis into who comprises a user's followers, friends or page views, these are usually *ante facto* analyses based on 'post metrics' or 'post performance' (this will be discussed at further length in the next section) – which means that it is usually only *after* the UGC has been posted that analyses can be performed to better assess who might comprise target demographics (which then can inform future content and post development). Of course, this does not mean that for-profit, non-profit and individual users do not have any sense of who is viewing their UGC. For instance, individual users, who might self-translate their UGC, know that, at a minimum, their list of *Twitter* followers or *Facebook* friends constitutes a very plausible target audience. This is also the case for non-profit and for-profit UGC: presumably most followers, friends or subscribers (*YouTube*) offer a glimpse as to who the core target audience might be. However, as individual OSM users can easily choose to 'unfollow', 'unfriend' or 'unsubscribe' as they please, these lists do not necessarily constitute a reliable indicator.

4.2.2 *Translating Tactile Modalities in OSM Branding*

Linear or traditional textuality (cf. Vandendorpe 2009) is problematized when we consider the ways in which tactile mobility has radically changed how users engage with texts.[7] While localization training does address how to adapt button and tab names to engage software users or video game users to take action, these activities initially meant interaction with 'non-mobile' hardware, such as a keyboard or mouse linked to a desktop or laptop computer. Tactile screens have changed this: by freeing users from additional hardware, tactility has ostensibly meant more mobility. As a result, OSM have incorporated tactile technology to engage users in unprecedented ways. Whereas in the early days of *Facebook*, users still 'clicked' via laptop keypads or mouses to 'like' a UGC post, now, given the pervasiveness of mobile tactility, users increasingly interact directly with the screen. This seems inconsequential for translation, but it has meaning, especially for the translation of social brands that are built on specific kinds of screen interaction. As Oswald (2012) argues, translation is the key to ensuring effective marketing of brands across the Internet. Setting aside the discussion on corporate powers and who really profits from effective translation, let us consider an example. In 2012, a new 'social discovery' dating application named *Tinder* became available and it quickly became one of the fastest growing dating applications on the market (Bilton 2014). While its geolocation search and match algorithms are worthy of interest in and of themselves (as they were the primary market differentiator from other online dating applications), here, specifically, it is the notion of 'swiping' that warrants attention for TS. *Tinder*'s brand is premised upon the action users take to select potential romantic partners: as photos appear on the screen, swipe right if you are interested, left if you are not. As the application grew in popularity, users increasingly spoke of 'swiping' to refer to time spent on *Tinder*. Here, the translation of 'to swipe' or of 'swiping' is not just a matter of ensuring the localized translation fits in terms of characters or spatial constraints (e.g. as with *tweets* that have a specific character-count) it has to engage the user on a *kinesthetic* level. In other words, the movement of 'swiping' is central to *Tinder's* brand. While some will speak of *zapper* or *glisser* (proposed French translations), these do not denote or prompt exactly the same action. The argument can be made: 'What does this matter, really'? If someone '*zaps*' in French or 'swipes' in English, is this a real translation 'challenge' or 'problem'? The answer is that it does matter. It matters in that translators (or localizers or crowdsourcers, case depending) must understand that what they are translating extends beyond previously taught modalities. Research in TS has long suggested that what translators translate necessarily goes beyond 'the text'; in this sense, these assertions are not revolutionary. Video game localization, for instance, is one key area in which some thought has been given to the user's kinesthetic experience (Bernal-Merino [2015] and Jiménez-Crespo [2013] give thought to 'cohesive interactivity' and 'web usability', respectively), but this rarely involves thinking about how this kinesthetic experience also intersects with cross-cultural branding and user engagement, as the *Tinder* example suggests. What is being considered here is not only a question of finding a lexical equivalent that would prompt the user to take the same or the appropriate action, but the connection between that action and the *marketing* of the product to international audiences (cf. Oswald 2012).

In a similar vein, in 2012, the photo-sharing application *Instagram* added a feature called 'the double-tap' (Panzarino 2012, online). This feature enables users to literally tap their tactile screen twice, in rapid succession, to 'like' a post. As soon as a user taps twice, a heart appears and disappears to show that the post has indeed been 'liked'. Although the term 'double-tap' doesn't seem to have gained the same mainstream notoriety as *Tinder's* 'swipe', the notion of 'double-tapping', as a form of social approval, became popular among *Instagram's* user base.[8] As with the *Tinder* example, we see then how a brand's terminology directly intersects with the user's kinesthetic experience and contributes to building that brand's identity. How would translators translating press material for *Instagram* translate the term 'double-tap' (noun and verb), for instance? Although some French-language users on *Instagram* have used the term '*double-taper*', the translation doesn't seem to have gained much currency elsewhere, for instance in hashtag indexing on *Instagram* or in French-Canadian press. Future research could consider how these 'kinesthetic social brands' are translated in other language pairs and the degree to which the translated terminology is adopted and used (this would intersect with studies in terminology and terminometrics).

In another case, Eid and Al Osman (2016) discuss the importance of touch in a paper on the topic of 'affective haptics'.[9] They claim that touch is a key element of human communication. Some OSM platforms have started to seriously consider how haptics, specifically affective haptics (i.e. those related to human emotion), can be integrated into OSM to enhance the user's experience and their engagement. For instance, the peer-to-peer network *Stress OutSourced* is a social application that 'allows anonymous users to send each other therapeutic messages to relieve stress' (Chung et al. 2009, online), thus leveraging affective haptics to create a social experience. In this case, the haptic and kinesthetic (the terms are sometimes used synonymously) experience is not necessarily part of the app's branding strategy, say, in the same way as 'to swipe' was in the *Tinder* example, but it does raise the question of how 'touch' is communicated across linguistic and cultural divides. For instance, if *Stress OutSourced* is used by international users, what words and haptic prompts are used to communicate empathy, relief and understanding? In this example, the insight of translators, if we take the view that translators are, to varying degrees, intercultural mediators, could be quite useful. Unfortunately, as Eid and Al Osman (2016) observe, the current literature on haptics is limited, dispersed in various disciplines and at a relatively embryonic stage in terms of theory and application. However, as research gains momentum in this area, localizers and translators can find ways of making their expertise relevant, be it by translating application interfaces that integrate haptics or by providing intercultural expertise in terms of 'translating' these haptic and kinesthetic experiences. This line of thought runs somewhat parallel to Bernal-Merino's (2015) argument that there should be more cohesiveness between verbal and non-verbal sign systems, interactivity and context with respect to the translation and localization of video games (and by extension, here, OSM applications and platforms).

OSM applications, such as *Tinder* and *Stress OutSourced*, and other OSM platforms are being increasingly used on mobile devices,[10] which means that the kinesthetic experience is central to the localization and translation of the overall product, be it the platform itself, the UGC, the application or platform marketing materials (ads for the applications and platforms), and FAQ/user guidelines. Further, as non-verbal cues (i.e., 'affective haptics', such as vibrations, force or motions) also become more common with digital technologies and in social media applications, this ground might be fertile for future TS research, especially for those TS researchers that already have extensive knowledge of kinesthetic communication, be it through their knowledge of sign languages (e.g. American Sign Language) and/or tactile writing systems such as Braille. For instance, how could tactility and kinesthetic prompts be used to communicate meaning in situations where a user has an impairment? And how could this be integrated into today's social media applications to increase accessibility to a wider-range of users? Moreover, how can a baseline understanding of kinesthetic interactivity be incorporated into translator training to help trainees better understand and resolve some of these challenges?

If social media is to be integrated into translation of a curriculum, consideration could (and probably ought to) be given to how tactile modalities impact not only the localization of the platform or application but also the social brand's marketing and distribution. It could be possible to envision training that incorporates collaboration between Web application development, mobile development and translation in the future. This collaboration could be done in the context of entrepreneurial projects (such as those reported by Chiose 2016), in internship programmes, or even in interdisciplinary seminars offered as a corollary to university training. This would follow in the line of pre-existing collaboration between language and computer science programmes, for instance, as in computational linguistics.

4.2.3 Translation and Hashtag Indexing

Hashtag indexing, as indicated briefly in Chap. 3, is another illustration of how linear textuality is further disrupted on OSM. Hashtags can place UGC in a variety of social media 'discussions' simultaneously (these discussions are commonly known as 'conversations' or 'self-narratives'[11] [Deutsch 2014] within the industry), sometimes with intended effects and sometimes with unintended effects. Therefore, to conceive of hashtags and social media content as 'paradigmatic' (Pym 2011a) is essential. Although he does not refer to hashtag indexing specifically, Pym's observations (*ibid.*, p.3, citing Nielsen 2006, 2008) are applicable here:

> No one reads a website from top-left to bottom-right – the normal reading patterns form a large T or F shape, as they eye scans across the top of the screen then moves down vertically [. . .] Linearity is relegated to the apocryphal. We find that, in the age of electronic language technologies, texts are increasingly used paradigmatically. And since they are used that way, they tend to be created that way. And it is perhaps only fitting that they are translated that way.

Some might overlook the vital role hashtags play in placing UGC in the appropriate 'conversations'[12] even in unilingual settings, let alone bilingual or bicultural ones. For instance, if someone were to translate *#throwbackthursday* (En) by *#rétrojeudi* (Fr), this would not place the French-language UGC in the appropriate 'conversation', as *#rétrojeudi* does not index as frequently as *#jeudirétro* or even the shortform *#TBT*.[13] As a result, this would mean that this particular UGC post might not be seen by as many users or create as much engagement.

Another example, this time taken from the *Instagram* account @ExploreCanada, also provides a compelling illustration of intentional hashtagging: in a bilingually captioned post featuring a picture of the *Collège François-de-Laval* (a school with historical significance) located in Quebec City, the English caption uses the hashtag *#ExploreCanada*, which indexes all content related to the @ExploreCanada account itself and, more broadly, to travel in Canada. Interestingly, *#ExploreCanada* is equally functional in *both* English and French (i.e. the lexical units are the same in form and in meaning), so one could assume translation of the hashtag in this case isn't entirely necessary. Yet, in the French caption (the English and French captions both appear simultaneously beneath the same photograph), the hashtag *#QuebecOriginal* is used in place of *#ExploreCanada*. This strategy, i.e. of 'translating' the hashtags within a bilingual caption, is particularly effective, because instead of using *#ExploreCanada* twice (which does nothing to increase post popularity or visibility since it is the same hashtag), a second 'translation' is added, which then indexes the post not only in both English and French social conversations, but increases the overall 'reach' of the post, that is to say the number of users that engage and react to @ExploreCanada's UGC.

This example, like the one that precedes it, demonstrates that the translation of hashtags requires a dynamic way of thinking about equivalence, where 'dynamic' refers at once to a form of 'functional equivalence', but also in a way that takes into account the paradigmatic nature of hashtags, as well as the importance of 'reach' in OSM conversations. Unfortunately, many translators who are unfamiliar with social media and hashtag indexing do not broach the translation of hashtags as broader units of meaning – they either fall into the trap of 'translating word-for-word' (as with the *#rétrojeudi* example) or of avoiding hashtag translation altogether. Exercises involving the translation of social media captions that use hashtags could help students familiarize themselves with frequently used hashtags (and hashtags that are abbreviated, e.g. #tbt) and invite these students to explore how indexing works. Even if trainees are not trained to an expert degree, in a situation where they would be called upon to translate social media content in a professional capacity later in their career, they would at least have a degree of familiarity and a deeper understanding of the implications of translating hashtags.

4.2.4 *Imparting Visual Literacy*

In Chap. 3, the hypervisual nature of contemporary OSM and UGC was addressed. These observations led to making an argument in favour of imparting visual literacy to translators (or semiotic literacy more broadly). Indeed, if translators are ever to be expected to translate 'intersemiotically', then they need to be 'fluent' in sign systems that go beyond the scope of natural languages. Unfortunately, few full-credit courses or modules on semiotics are taught as part of the core translation curriculum in the Canadian university survey, and it is likely that this is the case elsewhere as well. Students could take it upon themselves to register in semiotics courses, but these wouldn't be taught with an eye to professional translation practice, which would not remedy the situation. Research in TS at the graduate and post-graduate level continues to argue that translators 'must' go beyond 'the verbal' (cf. Oittinen and Kaindl 2008), but very few *practical* activities are assigned to *undergraduates* to effectively do this.

What could be envisaged, then, is a two-part undergraduate translation course taught over the full academic year that introduces foundational concepts in semiotics and multimodality, but with emphasis given as to how these intersect with translation. Visual literacy, for one, could be introduced to students as one example of 'multisemiotic' training. The term 'visual literacy' is used by Elkins (2008) to designate the competencies and skills necessary for understanding our increasingly visual world. He stresses that contemporary university education, more generally (not only in undergraduate translation or linguistics training), has given far too much attention to (verbal) texts, as the expense of equally rich and engaging visual content, or what he calls 'images' (*ibid.*, p. 3). His position aligns with the stance taken here: as much as undergraduate translation trainees are encouraged to think about the contexts and the effects surrounding translation praxis, they are rarely taught that translation is something that can happen beyond natural languages.[14] OSM affords the physical manifestation of what multisemiotic and multimodal translation might look like – and it is time for course/module designers and translation schools to seriously consider how to implement multimodal and multisemiotic training in the translation curriculum, lest students with backgrounds in media studies, communications or marketing take advantage of this opportunity before translation trainees.

Certainly, this proposal is fraught with underlying challenges. Course design and curriculum development is not the sort of process that happens in a vacuum. In Canada, as in many other countries, universities have to go through a complex process in order to obtain permission for creating additional or new courses, which usually comes about after extensive research on enrolment trends and programme evaluations. Elkins (2008, pp. 3–5) makes a case for the inclusion of visual competencies:

> It is amazing that college-level curricula throughout the world continue to be mainly text-based, with intermittent excursions into visual art and culture. [. . .] Since the 1980s the rhetoric of images has become far more pervasive, so that it is now commonplace in the media to hear that we live in a visual culture, and get our information through images. It is time, I think, to take those claims seriously. They need to be taken out of the graduate philosophy and history classrooms, and brought down the hall to the large lecture theatres where first-year students are taught the things university thinks are necessary for general education. It is time to consider the possibility that literacy can be achieved through images as well as texts and numbers.

Can current translator training programmes – at least those surveyed in Canada – purport to aptly train students if the material translated during their studies no longer reflect some of the 'texts' that are being produced in the 'real world' or do not adequately speak to the necessary literacies, skills and competencies required to properly analyse materials for translation? On-the-job training that comes at a latter career point and on-going professional development workshops (those that add to the 'basic' translator skillset) are certainly viable solutions for those currently in employment seeking to update or renew their skills, but they do not account for some of the newer generations of translators that are being trained up the ranks. No single programme can address all workplace realities or multidisciplinary avenues, but translation can no longer ignore how technology is commanding the imperative need for training that goes beyond 'the verbal'. If communication is increasingly being mediated through images, as Elkins (2008) and others (Oittinen and Kaindl 2008) have claimed, translator training must take note.

4.3 Social Media Metrics: The Value-Added of a Background in Translation After Graduation

Many terms exist to designate what essentially amounts to for-profit and non-profit entities (as well as some individuals) 'listening' to what OSM users are saying about them online. Commonly referred to as 'social media monitoring' or 'social media management and monitoring' (SMM), i.e. the 'active monitoring of social media channels for information about a company or organisation' (*Financial Times* 2016), the practice is also referred to as 'social media listening' and 'social media measurement'. The practice of SMM is increasingly popular across all market sectors, with government and public sector agencies even using SMM to better understand the needs and reactions of citizens in relation to government-produced documentation and policies. SMM is done using SMM tools (software and/or applications), with some of the most popular being *Facebook Insights, Hootsuite* and *Radian6*, although many more exist.

In most social media teams, whether internal or outsourced teams, SMM data is collected and analysed to enhance brand performance and visibility. Essentially, this is a means of targeting online content (UGC) more precisely and accurately to generate specific results, be it creating interest in a product or generating commercial sales. For a corporate brand, this might mean creating a new product or restocking a product following customer requests. For a politician, this might mean creating UGC that answers voter questions or that tackles a popular campaign policy. For a celebrity, this might mean engaging with fans and promoting a film or song or book. For a non-profit organization, this might mean monitoring to see whether programmes are effective and create engagement, and if so, what type of engagement. The list goes on. To be clear: SMM is not necessarily about generating profit, although in most cases it can assist in this vein. SMM is, essentially, a new(er) way of conducting market or audience research. In some ways, SMM is to OSM what reader–response theory might be to literature: it is a way of understanding the audience, intended or not. But, unlike literature, which tends to be fixed (i.e. determined), SMM allows social content producers (those who produce UGC) to 'redirect' the narrative. If one engagement strategy doesn't work, for instance if politicians are not garnering the public's support, or if a film is met with tepid reviews, SMM provides an opportunity to analyse why and to identify what went wrong, and to then adapt past, current and future UGC accordingly. Suffice it to say, the data generated by OSM, which SMM tools can subsequently 'translate' into empirical and qualitative analyses intended for various purposes, has radically changed some of the fundamental communicational power structures that have long existed between everyday citizens and those in positions of power. Corporations, celebrities and even university institutions, which were not always interested in what the 'crowd' how to say, are now paying attention – they are listening.

Of course, the question is what does SMM have to do with translation? As we shall see, there are indeed a few interesting connections to be made between SMM and translation. For instance, the 'simple' act of 'translating' social media data into qualitative analysis is already a form of knowledge transfer (knowledge translation) (cf., Göpferich 2010). In this section, the objective is to demonstrate how SMM training could be of value to translation trainees and what augmentation opportunities it can afford graduates of translation programmes.

The increasing use of OSM has meant that companies, organizations and individuals now have access to a wealth of online 'conversations' – conversations they might not have been privy in the past. This has created an entire industry sector focused on obtaining 'social intelligence' (i.e. the data) from SMM. Here, translators are positioned to be some of the most capable candidates in this market (this aligns with the concept of augmentation [Davenport and Kirby 2015], i.e. something 'machines' cannot do and that cannot necessarily be crowdsourced). With baseline knowledge of SMM tools, which could be part of an OSM and translation course, translators are a potentially valuable asset to any organization's listening strategy as they can monitor UGC 'conversations' not only in one, but two or even multiple languages. Further, their acquaintance with different cultural contexts makes them suitable to provide valuable feedback on how to use social intelligence to ultimately inform subsequent localization and translation initiatives. For instance, someone with a translation background can show a company where it makes sense to crowdsource translation and where it does not (e.g. professional translators for individual replies to customers versus crowdsourced translation for platform infrastructure). As translation-specific jobs dwindle in the Canadian public sector, once one of the key employers for professional translators in Canada, adding OSM competencies, such as SMM, to translation curricula, opens up a new set of employment options and makes the profession relevant in new ways. Whereas a unilingual employee could only 'listen' to 'conversations' in one language, the translator has the linguistic and cultural expertise to provide insight into at least two audiences, if not more.

In my own professional experience at *Library and Archives Canada* (LAC), I was part of the social media team that was in charge of creating OSM content for the department and of reporting on social engagement on various OSM platforms. Some of the colleagues in the team were unilingual, and, during the course of my contract, none of my immediate colleagues had a background in translation. Initially, I did not think my translation background would be of help in my monitoring duties. However, as the contract progressed, it became clear that having an understanding of how culture impacts translation equivalence was an advantage. For instance, when content was created in both languages (e.g. a *tweet* or *Facebook* post), but contained sensitive content for a given demographic, I was able to show this using the monitoring data, but *also* to propose a translation solution to address the issue (as the proverbs states: 'two birds, one stone'). This saved time for the team, as both monitoring and translation could be done by the same employee, as opposed to having to go through the usual two-step process of first analysing the data, then sending the data along with a translation request to another team within the department. Though this example is anecdotal, in recent years, a few of my students have graduated and found employment in similar sectors as well. Further research is required to track the number of translation graduates who have found employment in similar roles, but if my teaching and professional experience and that of my students' can be leveraged here, there is increasing evidence that translators possess many overlapping competencies to be effective SMM experts.

SMM skills represent a form of augmentation for job-seeking translators, but it also represents the value-added of human translators and translation expertise for companies and organizations at a time when MT, or the automation of translation more generally, gives the impression of being the 'better deal'. But what of the elite bilingual with SMM training? Unlike the elite bilingual, the translator affords additional value-added: not only can translators analyse social intelligence in two or more languages (something the elite bilingual could ostensibly also easily do), they can *also* translate UGC or propose translation strategies, something the elite bilingual might not be trained to do or even capable of doing.

Integrating SMM training into a translation programme would not necessarily pose as much of a problem as the integration of broader semiotic or visual literacies. This is mostly because translation technology courses could more or less seamlessly integrate SMM tools as part of the course content, that is, one or two learning components (e.g., a block of 10 hours within a module or course such as 'Translation Technologies' or 'Web and Translation') that address SMM tools.[15] While the degree of sophistication and generated social data varies widely between different SMM tools, the introduction of at least one SMM tool in the context of translator training can serve as a basis for most other tools (the essential metrics are the same, although capability and management options vary).

In a specialized translation course (TRA3534 Specialized Translation from English into French) offered at the School of Translation at the University of Ottawa (Canada) in 2011, one activity proposed to students was the translation of *Radian6*'s product information.[16] At the time, the site was only published in English and *Radian6* had not yet been acquired by *Salesforce*. For many students, this was their first foray into SMM technology (i.e. experimenting with a trial version of *Radian6* in order to better translate the related assignments). Even though the learning objective in this particular context was not to use *Radian6* itself, the students were happy to be made aware of SMM and the various tools used in the industry. In fact, after course completion, some of the students remarked that they now gave more consideration to employment opportunities related to social media, whereas this had not been the case prior to the course. Although the course evaluations obtained for TRA3534 2011 do not represent a statistical trend, the students' comments do suggest that they were keen and happy to be exposed to new employment options using their translation skills. They reported feeling that a degree in translation could be advantageous in communication jobs that required bilingualism as a prerequisite. This supports the argument that exposure to SMM tools is of benefit to students in the current economy (cf. Galt 2015).

4.4 Building OSM Communities of Practice Prior to Graduation: Leveraging OSM in the Classroom

The use of social media platforms in Canadian university classrooms is being increasingly monitored, regulated and studied. This, however, was not always the case. When *Facebook* was in its infancy, the notion that it could serve any pedagogical purpose seemed implausible (cf. Roblyer et al. 2010). Features were limited, membership was not public or universal and online connections usually had to be done through 'friending', which posed some issues with respect to student/professor confidentiality. As the platform evolved, however, new features, such as *Facebook Groups* and new privacy settings, were added, making it more realistic to consider the use of *Facebook* as a pedagogical tool. In 2009, when I initially inquired about obtaining permission to use *Facebook* in the translation courses I was teaching, no one within my department seemed to know of a clear guideline. The University of Ottawa did have licenses for campus-wide virtual learning environments (VLE) at the time (e.g. *BlackBoard*), but students reported general dissatisfaction with these tools: information retrieval was not user friendly or intuitive; the site occasionally crashed during peak times; and, perhaps more significantly, students did not feel the platform was an integral part of their social experience – that is, they did not consult it regularly and often forgot about its existence.[17] As a potential solution to these problems, I began to implement the use of OSM in the translation courses I taught.

In 2010, I presented part of my initial research on the integration of *Facebook* in translator training at the ninth edition of the *Voyages in Translation Studies* at Concordia University in Montreal (Desjardins 2010). Optimistic that the research would be received favourably, I was surprised to hear some of the criticism. Colleagues responded that *Facebook* was a commercial entity, an 'ad machine', and that using it in the classroom meant student exposure to unsolicited advertising and surveillance.[18] Interestingly, use of *Facebook* in all of my courses was done on a voluntary basis; in other words, students were not obligated to use the platform and they were informed of both data surveillance and target advertising. Succinctly, there was no hidden agenda on my behalf: *Facebook* was simply offered as an alternative to the campus-wide VLE that so many found unintuitive. In 2011, I reported findings that indicated that of the 200 undergraduates I had taught up until that point, only five had opposed using *Facebook*, stating that they either didn't have profiles ($n = 2$), which they later created, or that they had declined based on an ideological stance ($n = 3$) as their rationale (Desjardins 2011). To my mind, the colleagues that assumed student opposition and student 'harm' failed to recognize that students, in fact, were generally supportive and saw more benefit to using *Facebook* than not.

Like some of the colleagues at the *Voyages* conference, Fuchs (2014) makes a compelling argument, suggesting that *Facebook* is problematic because it masterfully veils surveillance and profit-making thanks to covert and overt advertising. To a degree, their points have some merit. This is why it is essential that students be made aware of how OSM functions 'behind the scenes': that is, to understand the free use of the platforms means trading in personal data. However, to suggest that any OSM platform is *more* fixated on profit than, say, campus-sanctioned VLEs is equally problematic. Companies that develop and license VLEs are for-profit. VLEs are a form of pedagogical surveillance in and of themselves (cf. Selwyn 2011): they track student log-ins, times of log-ins, student profiles, student performance and other metrics. In my experience, very few students were informed that campus VLEs generated this data. Also, little did students know that the VLE data was made 'public' to university professors, administrators and on-campus marketing teams. It is interesting how the issue of consent and surveillance pose a problem when OSM is the topic of discussion, and how the perception varies significantly when the topic turns to institutionally sanctioned VLEs.[19]

The position taken here is that OSM more directly aligns with social constructivist theories in education (cf. Kiraly 2000) than other 'institutionally acceptable' VLEs or alternatives, a position that is shared by other researchers as well. For instance, Kelm (2011, p. 505) affirms 'many principles of social constructivism coincide with the ways that social media enhances learning in our everyday lives'. He further states (*ibid.*, pp. 507–508):

> For social constructivists, knowledge is something that is constructed within a social context. People within a community help each other out, lend support, interact with one another, serve as shadow guides, and build on each other's progress. [. . .] In looking at the features of social media and innovative technologies, we see that their strengths coincide with the principles espoused by social constructivists. [. . .] technologies also enhance the shift from verbal communication to visual and verbal thinking. [. . .] All of this suggests that our implementation of social media and innovative

> technologies into our pedagogy correlates well with social constructivist thinking about learning in general. It is for this reason that there is a certain irony to the fact that educators sometimes feel that social media is a distraction to learning [. . .].

Since I initially started research on the topic of social media and translator training in 2009, many new OSM platforms have been launched and have increased in popularity (*Instagram* and *SnapChat* being two front-runners at the time of writing). While I have used *Facebook* with much success in my translation classroom, some educators, trainers and professors might have found success using other platforms (e.g. *YouTube, Twitter*, or *Tumblr*). If this is the case, it would be valuable to have data on this activity published in research.

For the moment, we can consider some of the ways using *Facebook*, notably, has appeared to be beneficial in translator training. I have argued elsewhere (Desjardins 2011) that the use of *Facebook* enhances the opportunity for disciplinary communities to be formed at the level of training. For translation trainees specifically, this means forging a classroom community centred on the discussion of translation. Such a community encourages students to see the value of networking (which is essential for anyone working as a freelance translator); to use translation metalanguage (cf. Delisle and Fiola 2013) in practice and discussion regularly; to expose trainees to media-rich environments (exposure to multimodal and multisemiotic texts); and to expose students to OSM more generally, which includes fostering critical thinking about these tools (i.e. OSM literacy). Moreover, professional translation praxis is, now, as localization and crowdsourcing so adequately illustrate, collaborative and digitized. Though translators have always collaborated to a degree (e.g. consulting with subject field experts, or terminologists, or clients), new technologies and digitization have created new types of workflow processes in translation projects, which require a command of digital and OSM competencies. The use of OSM in translator training, especially at the undergraduate level and for collaborative purposes, exposes students to the OSM platforms and the types of 'texts' they will likely have to incorporate into their professional practice at an early stage in their career development.

As more and more companies, institutions and individuals use social media as a 'voice', the demand rises for translators and UGC creators to be able to translate 'this voice' or 'social media presence', across linguistic and cultural barriers. For instance, the *Royal College of Surgeons and Physicians of Canada* has an in-house translation team that supports the Corporate Communications team in translating and adapting social media content, which is published in separate language feeds (English and French) on *LinkedIn* and *Twitter*. This example shows that competency in medical translation is insufficient in this context. *Tweet* translation requires translators to be able to convey content and to index content using limited character counts, appropriate hashtags, while simultaneously maintaining a tone that is appropriate for a corporate account of this nature. Translators who have never been exposed to these challenges prior to professional employ run the risk of finding this kind of work surprisingly difficult.

So while many arguments can be made for *not* using OSM in translator training, I would argue otherwise. This is not to say that a critical assessment of OSM platforms should not be made, but to insist on a general proscription of OSM in education on the basis of surveillance and profit generation does not put the student in a position of personal agency, where *they* get to make the decision. If we want to impart translator agency, then giving students the opportunity to voice their expectations and to participate in different learning initiatives is fundamental. As has been argued in other sections, social media are pervasive: given that the role of training is to prepare trainees for the marketplace that awaits them upon graduation, it follows that translation training, especially at the undergraduate level, must incorporate technological change and innovation into the classroom, whether this means using technologies in the context of practical translation activities (as the previous section argued for SMM tools) or as a part of the teaching methodology more holistically.

4.5 Conclusion

This chapter sought to discuss the various roles OSM can, should and could have in translator training in the context of undergraduate training. Understandably, curriculum design and undergraduate programme development is a complex process and one that is embedded in a contentious debate about what university education should and should not be in society. Because translation is a vocational pursuit, training, in whatever form it takes, must inevitably address the market. This does not mean espousing an uncritical stance; in fact, it is through the discussion of contemporary professional issues that some power structures within the market can be exposed and countered. However, this cannot be done if training does not take into account new social realities, such as the widespread use of OSM. For these reasons, the position taken in this chapter is that OSM must be integrated into translator training, if not only to ensure that graduates are marketable to employers, but also to ensure that translators possess the adequate skills necessary to critically think about the OSM platforms, UGC, non-verbal communication, SMM tools and the overall social landscape they will inevitably confront in professional practice.

Notes

1. The term and concept 'military, industrial, political complex' is also found in the work of American sociologist C. Wright Mills in his book *The Power Elite* (1956/2000). Giroux's contribution lies notably in how he applies this term and concept in a contemporary academic environment.
2. In some European countries, on-going professional development or continuing professional development (CPD) is compulsory in order to comply with industry standards and maintain accreditation. For instance, in the Netherlands, 80 hours of CPD are required over 5 years, an operational norm that has been in place since 2010 (Rogers 2015, p. 27).
3. At the time of writing.
4. And the hypothesis can perhaps be extended to other universities as well, although more research here is necessary.
5. 'Augmentation [. . .] means starting with what humans do today and figuring out how that work could be deepened rather than diminished by a greater use of machines. [. . .] We propose a change in mindset, on the part of both workers and providers of work, that will lead to different outcomes – a change from pursuing automation to promoting augmentation. This seemingly simple technological shift will have deep implications for how organizations are managed and how individuals strive to succeed. Knowledge workers [which include translators] will come to see smart machines as partners and collaborators in creative problem solving.' (Davenport and Kirby 2015, p. 60)
6. If a user's profile is private, presumably their audience is more limited, that is, limited to those that have been granted access. Conversely, if a user's profile is public, this means anyone with access to the OSM platform in question can see the content. Therefore, while a determinate audience cannot necessarily be identified in either case, the range of possibilities is significantly greater in the latter case.

7. Although Munday (2016) talks about multimodality in his chapter on new media, there is no overt mention of tactility or tactile screens, or how either may impact translation.
8. At the time of writing, the hashtag *#doubletap* has 16,426,269 indexed posts on *Instagram* (Instagram 2016).
9. An emerging field, which focuses on the analysis, design, and evaluation of systems that can capture, process, or display emotions through the sense of touch (Eid and Al Osman 2016)
10. 'A mobile device is a handheld tablet or other device that is made for portability, and is therefore both compact and lightweight. New data storage, processing and display technologies have allowed these small devices to do nearly anything that had previously been traditionally done with larger personal computers' (Technopedia 2016b: online).
11. The use of 'self-narrative' recalls Mona Baker's (2006) research on narrative theory in TS, specifically the concept of 'ontological narrative'.
12. The concept of an 'appropriate conversation' largely depends on where the user would like their content to be seen. For instance, an appropriate conversation could mean indexing a *tweet* that includes breaking news alongside other *tweets* that discuss the same news item (in Canada, the hashtag *#CdnPoli* is often used to index news stories that relate to Canadian politics and breaking news in this particular arena). Another form of 'appropriate' indexing might be to ensure that a post will be seen by a specific demographic, in which case the hashtags used might not necessarily connect content thematically, but rather strategically. For instance, on *Instagram,* the make-up artistry community will often use a variety of hashtags that have nothing to do with make-up per se, but that would likely be searched by, say, millennials, that is, a demographic that might buy the service or product these make-up artists promote. Other service industry professionals (e.g. personal chefs and nutritionists) and personal professionals (e.g. personal fitness trainers and life coaches) index their content similarly, that is to say they use hashtags that do not explicitly reference the content, service or product, but that would likely be searched by a target consumer.
13. This data is based on personal professional translation experience and social media analytics conducted over the course of a 6-month term contract at *LAC*, as part of the Web and Social Media Team.
14. Although the example is anecdotal, it is striking that when I ask my undergraduate students (who are enrolled in a first-year Introduction to Translation module or a General Translation module) whether they think images can be translated, they usually quickly answer no, only then to realize that subtitling, dubbing and localization are, in fact, instances where visual images are effectively translated.

15. This proposal runs parallel to Munday's (2012, p. 25) position: 'For instance, specialized translation courses should have an element of instruction in the disciplines for which the trainees are planning to translate – such as law, politics, medicine, finance, science – as well as an ever-increasing input from information technology to cover computer-assisted translation.'
16. I was the lecturer for this course and data provided in this section comes from the anonymous course evaluations given back to lecturers and professors after course completion.
17. Data and student commentary collected anonymously through course evaluations from 2008 to 2014.
18. This stance is shared by Fuchs (2014) who addresses the relationship between surveillance and *Facebook*.
19. For more on the topic of commercial surveillance, OSM and VLEs, cf. Weller 2007; Desjardins 2011.

CHAPTER 5

Translation and Social Media: In Professional Practice

Abstract Chapter 5 addresses the relationships between online social media (OSM) and the professional translation market, and, more specifically, how professional translators are leveraging OSM in creative – and sometimes surprisingly lucrative and beneficial – ways. The chapter lists some of the ways in which translators self-describe their work and their self-perceived role(s) on various OSM platforms, with emphasis given to activity on *LinkedIn*. Research in translation studies has sought to 'unveil' the very people – the translators – who have helped disseminate knowledge and culture such that they be seen and recognized for their contributions. While this chapter explores the positive aspects associated with translators' digital presence, it also calls into question the potential pitfalls of this 'digital visibility'. Could the translation *tweets, statuses* and other forms of user-generated content not also paradoxically contribute to the translator's invisibility?

Keywords Translation market · Professional translators · *LinkedIn* · User-generated content (UGC) · Translator's invisibility

5.1 Introduction

It has been acknowledged that a divide between theory and professional practice has existed for some time within the broader field of translation.[1] Some professional translators lament that translation theory is 'useful' for specific types of translation practice, such as literary translation, but not for

R. Desjardins, *Translation and Social Media*, Palgrave Studies in Translating and Interpreting, DOI 10.1057/978-1-137-52255-9_5

others ('Is Translation Theory Useful . . . ', 2011, online). Others remark that the problem lies in how translation theory is defined and used (*ibid.*). That professional translators (still) view translation theory as disassociated from their quotidian tasks is unfortunate, as theory offers a critical lens with which to refine one's professional skills (cf. Chesterman and Wagner 2002; Meyer n.d.). As Szczyrbak (2011, p. 80) states: '[. . .] voices can be [. . .] heard saying that translation theory is *interesting*, but *irrelevant* for practicing translators' (emphasis in original). From another viewpoint, that translation studies' (TS) theorists and researchers do not always acknowledge workplace realities in discussions on translation theory only serves to further this schism – a point Szczyrbak (*ibid.*) also speaks to. Valid reasons can explain the lack of overlap and collaboration: the scope of a given case study; the extent of one's professional and academic network; the myriad of niches within the larger translation profession which lead to professional and academic silos (cf. Gouadec 2007); the various national and legal jurisdictions that define translation differently across the globe, making standardization of practice challenging; and the (controversial, yet often overlooked) fact that some translation theorists have never or rarely translated professionally beyond the odd freelance contract. This is not intended as a reproach; it is possible that someone who has not extensively translated professionally is quite apt in their analyses of how translation functions within a social system or in their analyses of translated literature, for instance. And it does not mean that they are not capable translators. But it can indicate a lack of awareness as to what *effectively* happens in professional translation contexts on a *daily* basis, for instance, bearing witness to the dynamics of an internal translation team within a corporation; interactions with clients, superiors and stakeholders; workflow management; generating return on investment or how to make translation profitable; the integration of newer and more sophisticated translation 'tools' (software; applications); and even the phasing out of human translators altogether (cf. Delisle 2016). The question of 'theory' also depends on what researchers are trying to achieve when theorizing translation: even if a researcher has limited professional translation experience this does not negate their aptitude for critical analysis, as previously stated. The study of translation and the agents of translation can help establish guidelines for best practices, identify instances of poor practice, and further elucidate how translation occurs (or doesn't occur) in social settings, all of which are essential in professional practice.

In this chapter, the intent is to link translation theory and praxis with a particular focus on the connections between online social media (OSM) and these two areas. The debate, admittedly, is not inherently new, as the concepts of originality and visibility, to name only these two, has been ongoing. However, that does not mean that we cannot pose these questions in relation to OSM and see how this might (or might not) change previously held positions. Notably, this chapter will give critical consideration to the impact of OSM on the discourse[2] of professional translation produced by *practicing* professional translators. Building on previous discussions on translator agency and visibility, the argument is that OSM affords translators with a new means to *self-represent* within the larger marketplace (i.e. alongside other professions). Visibility has been seen (Venuti 1995; Chesterman and Wagner 2002) as an 'objective' to which professional translators should aspire; however, could this increased digital visibility on OSM have unintended effects? And if so, what are these effects and is there a way to counter them? Moreover, in what ways have OSM been leveraged by professional translators in the context of their practice? Has the use of OSM – such as blogs, professional forums and *Twitter* feeds dedicated to translation tips – been shown to be beneficial?

Further still, we might ask: has OSM created a more participatory translation community? OSM makes uploading, posting and sharing translator and translation of user-generated content (UGC) easier than ever, which means that now, the discussion of translation can go beyond academic or professional translation niches and silos, with stakeholders from other industries or experts in other fields weighing in – which might constitute a step towards what Venuti calls a 'translation culture' (Venuti 2013, p. 247). And while it is true that newsletters and other printed or 'traditional' documentation have also contributed to participatory culture in the past (cf. Standage 2013), the difference with today's OSM is their pervasiveness, their reach and their potential for contributing to viral trends. In other words, unlike the print or e-newsletter that reaches a pre-determined group of receivers, a professional translator who posts translation-related UGC on OSM can find their content reaching unintended audiences, and, in turn, having unexpected effects.

5.2 Professional Translation and OSM

Recourse to the presumably 'layperson crowd' for crowdsourced translation has generated some controversy (see Chap. 3), but the translation of OSM platforms has also shown just how vital translation is, regardless of the availability of *lingua francas*, otherwise such demands for translated (social) platforms would not exist. In a sense, although the demand for OSM in multiple languages has meant a rise in crowdsourcing and a potential threat for remunerated work, it has shown that a broad OSM user-base generally values, wants and needs translation, despite currently integrated or embedded automatic translation features (such as *Bing Translation* on *Facebook*) and the global dominance of English. The profession is at a crossroads: while some can choose to dig in their heels and view crowdsourcing and OSM as threats (which recalls some of the fear-based rhetoric regarding automatic machine translation in the mid- to later twentieth century), others can choose to view these phenomena as an opportunity for industry growth and increased professional recognition. Professional translators are now poised to make gains in the social media localization industry (as discussed with the concept of 'augmentation' [Davenport and Kirby 2015] in Chap. 4) – and here, localization is not used in the stricter sense of translating strings of text intended for software, websites or video games, but rather in the sense of contributing to a holistic cross-cultural OSM engagement strategy for brands, government affiliations and non-profit organizations. While cross-cultural communication seems to mystify some (non-translator) communication experts as a recent phenomenon, it is the very foundation of any translator's training. Cindy King (2010), a cross-cultural marketing expert, explains to her intended audience that localization (which she appears to equate with translation) is absolutely necessary to achieve 'successful' cross-cultural communication and she does so in a way that suggests this isn't common knowledge in her industry (*ibid.*, online):

> [...] the localization of social media communication goes deeper than cross-cultural people skills. Social media communication can be a little more challenging than other traditional forms of communication such as print communication or emails.

King also mentions that different cultures leverage the same OSM platforms differently. For instance, networks are forged differently on *Twitter*, job hunting is done differently on *LinkedIn* (she underscores the 'North American atmosphere' of the platform), and the cultural variations in professional and personal profiles abound (including picture selection, inclusion of credentials, etc.).[3] Interestingly, King also says that being aware of and adapting OSM UGC is 'much more than just translation'. Implicitly then, she seems to suggest that translation is somehow 'less' than her understanding of a 'more holistic' form of cross-cultural communication, which is a limited understanding of translation most trained and professional translators know to be false. The position taken throughout this book is that an OSM-savvy *translator* is in fact *far better* equipped to manage social media initiatives than the elite bilingual with a communications background (this argument builds on content discussed in Chap. 4). This is because translators have a value-added over professionals who 'only' have communications training. In other words, not only can translators understand linguistic and cultural nuances, they can also mobilize their translation skills to propose effective translation solutions in a given target language, whereas this is not always the case for those with a communications background who are unilingual, and, even in some cases, those who are elite bilinguals. This line of thought runs parallel to Gouadec's (2007, p. xvii; emphasis in original) assertions that while many people still think of translation as 'just' a matter of languages, it is in fact significantly more than that:

> It must be emphasized from the start that the **qualified** professional translator is a vital player, both economically and technically: professional translators are highly skilled technical experts, both on account of the contents they translate and of the various ever more sophisticated IT tools and software they must be able to use. They are in fact experts in multilingual multimedia communication engineering.

Of course, not all translators will find their niche working with OSM and UGC,[4] but this is nothing new: translators tend to find a niche to specialize in, whether this is medical translation, legal translation, scientific translation or otherwise. Thus, OSM and UGC, in a sense, simply constitute a newer market in which professional translators can gain significant ground given their linguistic, cultural, technical and analytical competencies.

Further, what the 2009 *LinkedIn* 'translation scandal' (see Chap. 3) showed, and this was in part thanks to the very visible outcry via translator UGC on OSM, was that translators tend to unite around the same challenges, thus in turn creating a community of practice with shared experiences. This indicates the participatory potential of OSM for the profession and the translation industry at large. Whereas translation has always been, to varying degrees, a collaborative endeavour, OSM has contributed significantly to creating new digital spaces of social and professional convergence for translators at all career stages. In the UGC that they share on platforms such as *LinkedIn*, translators have openly discussed some of the challenges that affect *all* translators, which include many of the topics Gouadec (2007, p. xviii) had already indicated to be commonplace:

> the general lack of consideration for their work, the complexity and technicality of the tasks involved, the impact of the ICT revolution on their working practices, the upheaval caused by the Internet, the industrialisation of the translation process and translating practices, market globalisation and job de-localisation, the increasing encroachment of language engineering applications, the rivalry between 'linguists' and 'technicians', the stringent requirements of quality certification, the fight for official recognition of a professional status (where this is not already effective), or even the fight for survival of the more 'cottage industry' translators.

In addition, translator-produced UGC has not only been crucial in fostering social and professional convergence among translators (i.e. *Facebook* groups or *LinkedIn* groups), it also provides unprecedented insight into the minds of translators (cf. O'Hagan 2011[5]). While different approaches have poked and prodded into translators' thought-processes – advances in eye-tracking analyses, neuroscience and think-aloud protocols (TAPs) have brought about significant contributions (cf. Kussman and Tirkonnen-Condit 1995; Bernadini 2001; Grucza et al. 2013; Tymoczko 2014; Watts 2014) – little has been said on what translators' UGC can contribute in terms of a better understanding of why translators do what they do, how they do it and how they talk about their work in online social settings, specifically on newer OSM platforms such as *LinkedIn*. Some might suggest translator UGC of this nature is simply a repackaged form of TAP, and the connection is logical. However, there are a few distinct and noteworthy differences: whereas studies based in cognitive studies, neuroscience and eye-tracking techniques require sophisticated equipment (which usually entails significant research and infrastructure funding), participant consent and ethics clearance (which are not always givens), the qualitative data (e.g. comments, user profiles, etc.) and quantitative data (e.g. post metrics, number of 'friends' or 'connections', etc.) that can be extracted from OSM platforms is far more accessible. Publicly available UGC is, by definition, publicly accessible (although there can be copyright constraints) and collecting UGC data is not as dependent on sophisticated technology as other forms of data collection. In fact, this is where social media monitoring (SMM) tools can be very useful for TS researchers and professional translators alike: not only do they track what is being said about a particular topic (through hashtag tracking, keywords and other searches), SMM tools can also track specific posts by topic and by platform and provide empirical reports for each search. And though this may change in years to come, using publicly available UGC does not pose significant issues with regard to ethics clearance, which in turn can speed up the research process. Thus, from the UGC that translators willingly share publicly on OSM, two significant areas can be further studied: (1) the discourse *on* professional translation *produced by* translators themselves, and (2) the commentary and thought processes of translators with regard to translation output more specifically. The second area does find overlap with studies involving online translator networks (cf. McDonough 2007; Perrino 2009; Folaron 2010b).

5.3 TS Research and Online Presence

Another area that warrants consideration under the rubric of 'professional practice' is the knowledge translation (cf. Göpferich 2010) of TS research via OSM platforms. OSM platforms are a space for the dissemination and discussion of new research within the field of TS. Some notable TS scholars have made extraordinary use of OSM to publish their research or to create forums for the discussion of TS research (Mona Baker and Anthony Pym are two forefront examples, both having websites and various social media accounts). Professional translation associations and TS associations have also started to come on-board. At the 2015 *International Association of Translation and Intercultural Studies*, a *Facebook* page was created so that participants could upload all sorts of UGC: status updates, audiovisual content (photos and videos), comments and links. On a surface level, this may seem innocuous, but it is significant. Some delegates even 'live-tweeted' the conference by uploading *tweets* about the conference presentations and activities as they were happening, which has been relatively unprecedented prior to the digital era (formerly, one presumably had to wait for conference proceedings to be published). These 'live-tweeting' and 'live-posting' activities even garnered interest from users that were not directly involved in the conference itself, but that seemed to have an interest in translation and TS.[6] As universities try to find ways of disseminating academic research in more cost-effective and engaging ways,

OSM initiatives have relevance. Not only do they afford one strategic method of disseminating research and updates about research to wider audiences rapidly, they also place academic research, and in this case, TS research specifically, within broader social discussions, especially when popular (or 'trending') hashtags are used. OSM can thus index (i.e. same type of indexing as hashtags) academic research in unexpected ways. For translation, especially, a profession and area of study that is often the 'victim' of being misunderstood, grossly simplified and invisible, OSM provides a new voice. In a sense, the 2009 *LinkedIn* 'translation scandal' also exemplified this: professional translators and TS researchers engaged in the discussion of crowdsourcing translation (cf. Dolmaya 2011) and other 'voices', from beyond the field of translation, also contributed their viewpoints.

The use of OSM to disseminate TS research also has the added benefit of 'crossing' both tangible and symbolic borders, which might increase consilience between otherwise isolated TS research communities and professional circles. For instance, not all university or training institutions have the same on-campus resources (libraries, electronic hardware, free WiFi access, etc.) or licensing agreements, particularly when institutions are compared on an international level. This can mean that some translation researchers, trainees and instructors have 'less' access to trade magazines, scholarly publications and other relevant materials. While OSM alone cannot fill this gap this entirely, a *tweet* about a new publication in TS or a *Facebook* post about an upcoming conference has the potential to reach audiences that might not have been attained through more 'traditional' channels. Equally important is the fact that UGC is not necessarily constrained by institutional firewalls: virtually anyone with Internet access who wishes to follow a research institution or academic publisher on *Twitter* or *Facebook* can.

In recent years, research within TS has increasingly emphasized the multidisciplinary and interdisciplinarity connections that have been made with other disciplines (Snell-Hornby et al. 1994; Duarte et al. 2006; Snell-Hornby 2006; Munday 2012). However, research can, like professional practice, be insular in nature. Shouldn't greater interdisciplinarity also involve the inclusion of professional and individual voices? Of those who, for geographic or institutional reasons, might not be able to contribute through traditional research channels? OSM could be increasingly leveraged in the knowledge translation and dissemination of TS scholarship.

Certainly, the idea of freely publishing (either through open-access licensing or through individually produced UGC), uploading and sharing TS research on OSM[7] raises a few issues. First, scholarship should ideally be peer-reviewed and assessed rigorously prior to publication and dissemination, which is not something that is a guarantee for all UGC purporting to be of scholarly quality.[8] Second, copyright law and fair-trade agreements cannot be overlooked. In recent years, OSM platforms have been far more observant and strict with the dissemination of copyrighted materials (*YouTube*, for instance, has warned users of copyright infringement and provides tutorials on fair use ['What Is Fair Use' 2016]). Third, the dissemination of scholarship online also poses the same issue as crowdsourcing: when anyone can do it, who are the real experts? A solution might be to explore how OSM applications can be integrated into pre-existing academic platforms. Are there ways of connecting social media feeds to particular journal titles or publishers? Can translation journals increasingly try to publish in open-access formats?

One example of a hybrid solution is that of *What's Trending in Translation Studies* ('What's Trending in Translation…' 2015), a Taylor & Francis portal that includes the online journal format, but also combines social media buttons that redirect to a *Facebook* page and *Twitter* feed.[9] The aim is as follows: 'To make it easier for you to find the latest, most popular research in Translation Studies, Routledge have put together this virtual collection featuring the most popular online research in Routledge journals. The articles included in this selection are free for you to read online.' This is a good example of how to maintain high publishing standards (as the publishing house still reviews submissions according to specific standards), while also placing recent research in more accessible social contexts. One social feature that connects a social conversation to TS research is that of the inclusion of a *Twitter* button on the publisher's website. This button, which redirects the user directly to the publisher's *Twitter* profile, makes it possible to quickly see what is being *tweeted* about with regard to linguistics and translation research. Figure 5.1 shows an example of a recent tweet that acknowledges TS scholar Mona Baker:

Although not all Routledge content is accessible via this portal – for the most part, it appears as though the virtual collection showcases very recently published content exclusively – the move towards greater online accessibility is welcomed, as is the inclusion of social features.

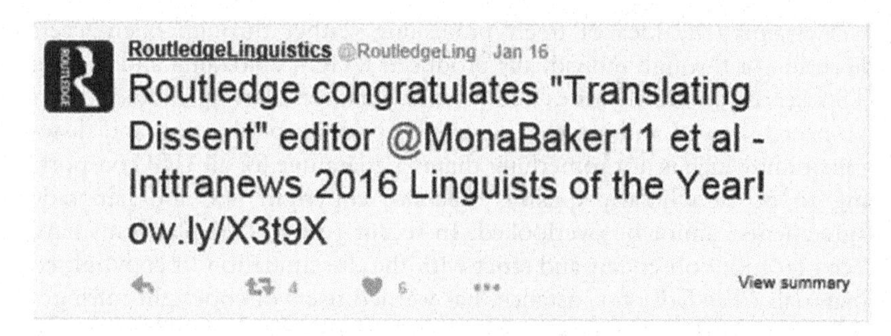

Fig. 5.1 An example of a Tweet that places a TS research in larger social conversations. Engagement can be monitored by the number of retweets (signalled by the number next to the rotating arrows) and the number of 'likes' or 'favourites' (signalled by the number next to the heart icon)

In a somewhat related fashion, if a researcher wanted to see how wider online audiences were engaging with their research or their UGC, they could set up a personal SMM account. Much like SMM for corporate brands, for-profit/non-profit organizations and institutions, individuals can track their own personal social media feeds to see how other users are engaging with their content. Some might view this as a corporatization of research, as researchers might be tempted, then, to react according to what is popular, trending or financially lucrative instead of producing research that is not motivated by financial or symbolic capital gain,[10] a perspective that would fall in line with some of Fuchs' (2014, 2015) observations.

In introducing how social media can have an impact on practice, be it in professional or research practice, a number of questions and ideas have been put forward. This chapter's scope does not allow for an in-depth exploration of all of these questions, but it will consider two key topics in greater detail: the 'new visibility' that OSM affords and, paradoxically, the 'new invisibility' that OSM creates.

5.4 The 'New' Visibility

The topic of translation and translator visibility attracted significant interest after the release of Lawrence Venuti's book *The Translator's Invisibility: A History of Translation*, which was originally published in 1995, with a second edition following in 2008. This is not to say that translator status had not been peripherally addressed prior to this, but this was the first significant contemporary publication that addressed the topic head-on, arguing that the translator should in fact have the same status, not just in discourse but in some legal and commercial capacities, as the author.[11] Translators, throughout history, have been responsible for the circulation of literature and knowledge. However, by making translations 'fluent', they have 'masked' the process of translation that creates the illusion that the target text (TT) is in fact a source text (ST). For instance, how many undergraduate students take philosophy courses in contemporary arts and humanities programmes without once problematizing the fact that Plato or Aristotle did not write in English?

Building on Venuti's work, other studies have shown how copyright law further marginalizes the translator and confines their work to a secondary status (Basalamah 2009), which also contributes to the 'problem' of invisibility. Copyright law, in some cases, can make the very act of translation impossible, thus preventing the dissemination of content and creating power imbalances. Presumably, if a work (e.g. a book, blog, or legal document) is originally written in English, today, and copyright law prevents or limits translation into other languages, especially into minority languages,[12] then this means English speakers/readers are then put in a position of power over those who require translation but that need to work through a legal system to obtain said translated versions. Another power structure surfaces when we consider how translators must 'ask permission' for translation rights, even if now translation is seen as 'a work in the legal sense' (Basalamah and Sadek 2014, p. 400): 'However, because of the need for an original, a translation is a secondary or derivative work and must therefore get the blessing of the author of the original, so to speak, before being undertaken.' Thus, it is not only through discourse on translation that translators and translation are made invisible, it is also through the processes that emphasize 'transparency' and 'fluency', as well as through the various legal structures that continue to view the translator and translation as secondary to and derivative of the author and 'original'.

Yet, as Basalamah and Sadek astutely remark (*ibid.*, p. 400), OSM and UGC have come to significantly disrupt the notion of 'derivative works' (in which translation is subsumed), which, as we shall see, has implications for translator visibility, and for empowerment as well:

> As it continues to break down barriers for the creation and dissemination of information, this interactive and networked medium [i.e. the Internet] is

> proving that creation and innovation can be better nurtured by collection and recursive (hence, translational) activities than by legally imposed monopolies. [. . .] Today, the Internet is being fed more and more user-generated content (UGC), most of which is derivative (mirroring translation), in the sense of being heavily dependent on pre-existing materials that are copied, modified and combined to create something new and original. [. . .] It is the same challenge to the notions of authorship and originality that we are witnessing today with blogs, forums and platforms such as YouTube, because they have made it exponentially easier for anyone to become a creator and producer of content, thus also reigniting the debate about translation.

OSM and UGC have effectively provided another lens with which to reconsider the 'derivative' status of translation. This debate is not inherently new, granted: the concept of originality – and by extension, re-writing – in relation to translation has been discussed through the lens of literary refractions (cf. Lefevere 1982/2004), gender politics (cf. Chamberlain 1988/2004), literary translation (Venuti 1998) and copyright (Basalamah 2009), to name only these few examples. But as Basalamah and Sadek underscore, it is the explosion of digital technologies that are changing the discussion. If all UGC is a form of translation (in a broader sense) or derivative, how can originality be defined in light of this? In his book *Free Culture,* Lessig (2004, p. 184) argues that 'capturing and sharing content [. . .] is what humans have done since the dawn of time'. Translation, in essence, is one way humans capture and share. So with translation occurring increasingly on OSM, what we are now facing is an unprecedented degree and speed of 'capturing and sharing': not only can content circulate rapidly regardless of linguistic barriers (a first level of 'capturing and sharing'), but content can also quickly spread on various digital platforms in seconds, for instance, from one social account to another, or from one platform to another (a second level of 'capturing and sharing'). As the law evolves to match current content production and the *speed* at which content can and does circulate, it will be interesting to see how existing copyright laws will be revised to account for new forms of UGC that are increasingly difficult to monitor and control (for instance, *regrams* or *latergrams* that do not cite the original *Instagram* post from which they were copied; *Facebook* shares that do not credit an original user or producer of the post; and blog content that is never monitored for plagiarism; or the translation of

UGC and its use by bilingual users without consent or permission). Of equal significance will be how such laws may or may not restrict creators (a group in which translators can be included), a topic that is also central to Lessig's analysis in *Free Culture* (2004).

With regard to content creation and dissemination, the concept of self-translation is equally thought-provoking: more and more bilingual OSM users are relying on their own translation 'skills' to disseminate content within their multilingual, multicultural networks. What happens when an author self-translates a section of their own work and posts this content on OSM? And shares it? Such activity could result in breach of contract with the publisher or copyright infringement, even if the original work is that of the author. This does apply in traditional print media as well, but, as previously stated, the major differentiator is the medium: online activity is much more difficult to regulate and monitor given the sheer abundance of UGC and the speed at which it can proliferate. In addition, this says nothing of what to do with regard to 'ephemeral' or timed content (i.e. posts that 'disappear' after a given amount of time) such as that found on *SnapChat*, for instance. In short, OSM and UGC are essentially the 'wild wild West' of copyright, originality, derivative works and authorship.

Implicit in the discourse on translator/translation (in)visibility is the notion of victimization, a point that Balasamah and Sadek (2014) also address. Many translators deplore the lack of recognition and pay in some areas of their work, yet they continue to work in these conditions without too much contestation. Translators are victims of the law, the power structures (institutional norms, workplace policy, etc.) and the discourse that perpetuates the view that translation is 'less than' (*ibid.*, p. 400). Here, again, OSM might offer a viable avenue to counter this discourse. OSM has been argued to be a mechanism for social change. Social change occurs when an existing social order or paradigm is disrupted in favour of new social order. Social change can occur to varying degrees and can impact behaviours, institutions, relations or norms. Currently, the 'social order' in professional translation is that the translator is almost by default invisible or 'less than'. Here, the argument is that OSM affords a way to counter the current order, in favour of a new visibility.

Previously, translators could not really 'talk back' to the actors that relegated translators and translation to a secondary status. For instance, at the time of writing, the Canadian Translation Bureau (the most significant employer in the industry in Canada) is phasing out a number of human translators in favour of opting for machine translation, which includes the use of a tool called *Portage* ('Online translator helps...' 2016, online). Whereas in the past the backlash from professional translators might have been equally strong, it might not have found an easy media outlet. However, many professional translators in Canada were quick to mobilize and use social media to voice dissent and frustration with the arrival and implementation of *Portage*. These translators, then, were not 'invisible' or 'voiceless': their *LinkedIn* updates, *tweets* and *Facebook* posts give them the opportunity to voice the value-added of human translator competencies and, ostensibly, 'to fight back' in relation to the Bureau's decision. And this sharing of dissent can be proven empirically: in the first 7 days following *Le Devoir* publishing of Delisle's (2016) article criticizing the Translation Bureau's downsizing in favour of automation, the article was shared 517 times on *Facebook* alone, which constitutes relatively significant post performance for this kind of content.

OSM also radically changes professional networking within industries. For instance, translators, like many other professionals, can now use professional networking sites such as *LinkedIn* to represent themselves in a professional capacity (no need, necessarily, for an HR 'middle person'). Whereas before, résumés were largely seen as confidential documents, today, thanks to OSM platforms, publicly available professional profiles have now become the 'new order'. Though it is true that translation and translator forums have existed for some time (*ProZ* being a popular example), affording translators with varying degrees of professional self-representation (translator profiles, blog posts, Q&As), sites such as *LinkedIn* place translator profiles within larger networks of professionals, thus placing translation 'on par', at least in terms of social networking, with other creative and language-based industries – and even beyond to other industries. If online social networks are a new way of gauging a professional's worth – in the same vein as *likes* and *followers* being a new form of symbolic capital – then those translators who have amassed networks of 500+ connections (e.g. on *LinkedIn*) are examples of capable social networkers. In other words, translators who are capable social networkers are able to make themselves *visible*. Professional translators can use social networking and can produce UGC to address topical issues on their terms. Going back to the example from the Canadian Translation Bureau, some of the press items related to the launch of the *Portage* tool made it seem as though human translators are now redundant, which contributes to the general perception that translation is 'just' about 'swapping' lexical items (Delisle 2016). The irony is that this perception, that of translation being an activity that can be fully automated, is being promoted by one of the most prominent employers in the Canadian translation industry. Thankfully for Canadian professional translators, they can counter this perception by leveraging OSM and by providing a different viewpoint: that *human* translation and *human* intervention in the translation process both still have significant value-added in today's market.

Professional translators who choose to become *LinkedIn* members (base subscriptions are free at the time of writing) are able to create their profiles themselves (without a pre-determined template exclusively for 'translators'). This means that they can list any of the tasks and skills they view as being central (or even peripheral) to their translation practice, which might serve to counter outsider perceptions that translation only involves specific language skills. In a review of my own *LinkedIn* network, most professional translators do include 'translation' as a skill; however, they also include a myriad of other skills such as project management, terminology, social media, research, data mining, analytics, teaching, search engine optimization, grant writing, leadership, intercultural communication, corporate communication, media relations and editing. Of course, it is no secret to most professional translators that translation is only one of the many skills deployed in one's daily work. But, what is striking on *LinkedIn*, and what seems to contradict the assumption that most non-translators view translation as 'only' about interlinguistic translation (cf., Desjardins 2013b) – at least in Canada, anyway – is the fact that these non-translator *LinkedIn* members can endorse a translator's *other* skills. So not only do non-translator members endorse translators' translation skills, they *also* endorse (thus, presumably, *acknowledge*) translators' *non-translation* skills (e.g. corporate communication, management, leadership, data mining, etc.). Therefore, activity on *LinkedIn* suggests a paradox about the discourse on invisibility and the limited, more popular definitions of translation outside the professional and academic circle of translation: although translation is at times perceived and framed as being 'only' an issue of interlinguistic transfer (cf. *ibid.*), activity in professional social networking seems to suggest otherwise, first by how translators represent themselves, but also in the way that *other* professionals (non-translators) endorse translators. For instance, while any translator (or any professional) can self-describe as being competent in the areas of 'research' or 'terminology management', this self-assessment of skills only goes so far, as no one else has vetted this competency. However, if a former client or superior or colleague, whose credentials can also be verified and traced back via their profile, provides the endorsement, then this would suggest that indeed the translator possesses some degree of mastery in a given area. Moreover, implicitly, this endorsement suggests that the endorsers *acknowledge* that the translator can possess skills and competencies that are beyond 'translation'.

At the time of writing, no systematic revue of *LinkedIn* data (quantitative and qualitative) exists in relation to the skills translators self-report as having (self-assessment) or in relation to the endorsements they receive within the translation industry or outside it. Such a study would have significant merit as it would lend empirical weight to the assertion that contemporary translators possess many skills that suggest market versatility. In addition, this data could serve to support revisions to legal provisions that continue to frame translation activity as derivative or secondary: when additional competencies are required to render a work in another language (let alone to create/re-create UGC on various platforms), there is in fact *new* labour that is being generated (cf. Rogers 2015) and that would warrant legal protection and appropriate compensation.

But perhaps more fundamentally, the profiles of professional translators on *LinkedIn* underscore that translators are no longer invisible. In the way that translators can now promote their freelance practices, in the way that they can now network with other professionals, in the way that they can self-describe what they do and how, OSM have given contemporary translators a voice and an unprecedented level of agency. Translators' notes and prefaces have historically given translators a means to be read or 'heard', but this was only for the readers of a specific translated text. Because OSM has a significantly wider reach, what translators say about translation, their profession and their process on OSM (i.e. their UGC) has a higher likelihood of making an impact in other professional circles and beyond.

While the goal here is not to endorse the use of *LinkedIn*, hopefully the case for using social media as a tool for promoting translator agency, relevance, visibility and accountability has been sufficiently made. OSM can contribute directly towards Venuti's (2013) idea of a 'culture of translation' given that they not only give translators a voice, but also provide a degree of visibility in the sense of *visual* and auditory representation as well: *LinkedIn* profiles also include multimodal components, such as profile pictures, video blogs and soundclips – features most translator prefaces and notes of the past could not provide.

The idea of 'translator profiles' is also interesting. As work in TS emphasizes the importance of profiling translators to better understand who the actors (agents) of translation activity are (i.e. sociological approaches in TS, cf. Gouanvic 2005; Heilbron and Sapiro 2007; Simeoni 2007; Wolf and Fukari 2007), online social networks provide great insight: data on *LinkedIn* (which is generally public depending on a user's parameters; see earlier comments about public UGC) can indicate how translators converge to form networks and around which professional poles they tend to gravitate. Moreover, information on academic and professional backgrounds can also be gleaned.

In short, the argument is that online professional social networking is one way to counter the invisibility of translation. By becoming visible on OSM platforms, be it by creating their own professional profile or by contributing UGC on translation and the profession, they are contributing to a new discourse that frames translators not as victims, but as engaged professionals; that frames translation not as a derivative of lesser value, but as a necessary means of cross-cultural communication, in the way that King (2010) and other social media experts advocate.

5.5 Translation Quality and OSM: #Invisible

In this section, further consideration will be given to translation quality with regard to OSM. It would appear that translation quality in the context of OSM content most often refers to translation (i.e. process, and, in some cases, product) being 'invisible', which is similar to the 'zero-time' effect discussed by Charron (2005) in the context of localization projects. As technological advancements speed up the translation process, Charron argues that this creates the illusion that translation happens simultaneously with the production of the original/source content, so users of the translation come to expect simultaneous, high-quality output in no time ('zero-time') (*ibid.*). Applying this to translation and OSM, content that is deemed 'good quality' and that has been translated usually makes no explicit mention of the translation process, the time required for the translation and the translators; that is, good translation = invisible. This is particularly the case for social media accounts that choose to create two different and separate accounts for each language in which they produce content (e.g. *Library and Archives Canada* [LAC] and *Bibliothèque et Archives Canada* [BAC] two separate *Twitter* accounts for English and French). Ironically, then, just as OSM affords a new visibility to the translator as subject, they can also erase or mask translation to varying degrees.

As has been previously explained, hashtags are a way of tracking popular conversation topics on OSM. It follows then that hashtags afford a new way of tracking what the 'crowd' is saying about translation more specifically. SMM tools can yet again offer more insight into what is being said about translation and by whom, and it would be interesting for future studies to conduct research of this nature. For instance, by using an SMM tool such as *Radian6* or *HootSuite*, researchers can restrict parameters (i.e. search for a specific set of hashtags; create SMM profiles) to see on which OSM platforms translation is being discussed more frequently, how and by who, or to see what topics and other hashtags tend to coincide with social conversations related to translation.

In addition to being an efficient way of tracking social conversations on the topic of translation, SMM is also one way of assessing translation quality on OSM. For instance, in Canada, most government departments have bilingual social media accounts that tend to be structured according to one of the two following options: either there is one account that publishes alternate English and French content (alternating posts or bilingual captions), or there are two completely separate accounts for each official language. Who is responsible for translating the UGC varies according to the government department (some departments have internal translation teams, while others outsource their content to the Canadian Translation Bureau, while others may employ freelancers or term-contract employees. In more recent developments, a new translation tool, the previously mentioned *Portage*, is being implemented for streamline translation within the Canadian public sector ['Online translator helps…' 2016]). What SMM can track in terms of engagement is how users within the larger OSM community respond to and/or engage with the original UGC (ST) and the translated UGC (TT). Ideally, engagement should be similar for both languages, regardless of the direction of the translation (i.e. the content should be engaging in both languages to generate the same engagement metrics). However, statistically, there are fewer Francophones in Canada compared to Anglophones, so it does follow that engagement metrics will always be lower in French (there are SMM parameters that can be adjusted so that analyses only focus on Canadian data; however, if one wanted to analyse activity for other demographics, SMM parameters can be reset accordingly). As a general rule, the idea is to generate at least *some* engagement in both languages for the same UGC post.

Figures 5.2 and 5.3 show two versions of the same post, one in French which was published on the French BAC *Twitter* feed and the other in English which was published on the English LAC *Twitter* feed. According to the data included in these *tweets*, the LAC and BAC social media accounts accrued a relatively strong following for a government department, which is indicated by the overall number of followers for both accounts (16,823 followers). It should be noted that these data were retrieved using SMM tools. What these two figures also illustrate is the user engagement based on language. In Figs. 5.2 and 5.3, the English UGC does have more engagement (more likes [2] and retweets [3]) than the French (which has one *retweet*), yet the discrepancy between each post's performance (i.e. level of engagement) is minimal. This suggests that the post was equally 'successful' (similar engagement) regardless of the official language used. Moreover, users did not report or comment on the translation, which suggests that readers of the post were

Fig. 5.2 Example of a tweet from Bibliothèque et Archives Canada's Twitter account (French)

Fig. 5.3 Example of a tweet from Library and Archive Canada's Twitter account (English)

satisfied. Engagement (or response) metrics can provide insight as to what is deemed to be of quality with respect to the translated content.

A number of models for translation quality assessment (TQA) do exist (cf. Brunette 2000; Williams 2004), though what constitutes 'quality' in translation varies extensively and has generated a degree of controversy in the field (Colina 2008, 2009; Mateo 2014). According to Martínez Mateo (2014, p. 73), a 'successful' TQA model is premised upon three key steps: defining the concept of 'quality'; establishing a methodology for measurement; and finally, the assessment itself. While the concept of 'quality' likely varies for the translation of UGC as much as it does in other types translation practice, what is significant about SMM tools is that they can provide a 'ready-made' measurement methodology and measurement metrics. For instance, if 'quality' in OSM translation is defined more or less by the same parameters attributed to good post performance more generally, then a 'good' UGC translation would be one that generates equal engagement (e.g., equal number of *likes*, or *retweets*, or *views*) across all linguistic accounts or bilingual and multilingual content. The data generated by SMM thus provides an empirical method to measure quality as defined by the strength of engagement. In addition, SMM can also track qualitative feedback from users, subsequently adding another dimension to overall TQA. Comment and reply features, on *Facebook* posts for instance, or reply features on *Twitter* all give users the opportunity to provide real-time feedback for translated content (just as much as they do for any UGC), and SMM can provide this information in the form of metric reports. If a post performs well empirically (i.e. a high number of *likes, shares, views*, etc.) and qualitatively (i.e. no negative comments or user backlash; or, conversely, positive comments), then one can hypothesize the translation was generally satisfactory, and thus of 'quality' or 'fit for purpose'.

SMM analysis in TQA is rather interesting, because it also enables social media teams to adapt 'poorly' translated content (i.e. content that is not engaging or that has received negative commentary) in real time. If SMM data suggest a translated post is under-performing in comparison to its original version, the social media team can revisit the translation to edit, delete or adapt accordingly. For instance, on *Facebook*, all posts can be edited simply by clicking the 'Edit' button and making necessary changes. Edits are tracked, meaning that users can consult earlier iterations of the post prior to being modified. Another solution is to delete the 'poorly performing' post, and resubmit a new version altogether. In this scenario, users are not notified of the deletion.

SMM ensures that strategic translation choices can be made and adjusted, and thus, that 'quality' is nearly always achieved. For instance, if a post is criticized by users of being poorly translated in the comments section, a social media team can track the commentary and make the necessary changes. After the changes are made, the social media team can continue to monitor the post to see how users react. Within the social media team at LAC, if a post's performance was underwhelming in *both* official languages (i.e. source and target UGC), the conclusion was that the topic of the UGC was simply not of interest to the user base (i.e. the audience). If post performance was underwhelming in only one language, then discussion would follow as to whether or not a translator could have mobilized other strategies (such as using other hashtags or keywords) to engage that specific language demographic. This is not to say the translator was necessarily at fault or that translation was the root cause of 'poor quality', but rather that in the context of UGC translation, if content is not creating user engagement, adjustments may need to be made. Moreover, as SMM analyses increasingly track responses to translation, trends can be identified to further inform subsequent translation strategies (here, we can recall the example in Chap. 4 on the topic of hashtag translation and how #jeudirétro was a more 'strategic' choice because it indexed more frequently than #rétrojeudi). As the production of UGC continues to grow across market sectors, translation in this area will as well. Consequently, there will be a need to establish what constitutes 'quality' in the translation of UGC to guide practice. Here, SMM tools provide one way to rethink TQA methodologies in the digital era.

However, 'quality' in this context appears to be a double-edged sword: when UGC is uploaded and generates significant engagement (i.e. good post performance), this is seen as 'quality' UGC; conversely, UGC that performs poorly, sometimes due to an issue related to the translation process (e.g. mistranslation of a hashtag, awkward lexical choice, etc.), is seen as being of lesser quality. Therefore, to draw a parallel with Venuti's work in literary translation, quality UGC translation usually involves 'naturalness' (pleasing 'the mainstream') at the expense of visibility that might call more attention to the translation process or the ST itself ('foreignness'). While a novel and a *tweet* are two very different text types, with different purposes and internal structures, Venuti's 'naturalness' and 'foreignness' still have relevance in an OSM context.

To further illustrate, let us return to the LAC/BAC example. Ironically, although Figs. 5.2 and 5.3 are the tangible products of a translation process (ST and TT) they also mask this very process and make it appear as though bilingual UGC is 'magically' uploaded simultaneously – an observation again similar to that found in Charron (2005). The fact that *Library and Archives Canada/Bibliothèque et Archives Canada* UGC is published in separated linguistic feeds and on two separate linguistic accounts might contribute to the public's perception that the *tweets* are in fact *not* the result of translation (i.e. translation becomes invisible). As with localization methods that seek to 'erase' translation and make content appear as though it was always intended for its target locale, many social media teams employ a similar strategy in the creation and curation of UGC (i.e. 'quality' = illusion of no translation). Multilingual brands, for instance, want to seem as though all their regional accounts have personalized/localized content, or at the very least, that their brand has the same impact regardless of the language in which the UGC is produced. Maintaining different feeds and accounts is one way to ensure fewer comparisons between source UGC and target UGC are made by users, which is strategic from a marketing perspective, but unfortunately adds to the misconception that translation of UGC is instant, easy and seamless. Many companies rely on social media management tools (such as *HootSuite*) to create and stock UGC in advance of the publishing date (i.e. the date a post or *tweet* goes 'live') to allow for revision, translation, fact-checking and other various quality checks. So while the *perception* is that of translation happening on OSM in 'real time' (akin to automatic machine translation), this is hardly the case. As other parts of this book have shown, translating UGC is not exclusively a matter of code-switching lexical strings: hashtag indexing, adaptation based on SMM metrics (see above), and, to a degree, the localization of UGC are all elements that, when compounded, can significantly impact translation turnaround times.

The literature on translation quality, OSM and appropriate UGC translation strategies is quite limited. In fact, one of the only comprehensive texts on the subject is in relation to *tweet* translation. In their work, Hamilton and Lavallée (2012) collected approximately 1750 *tweets* and, based on their analyses of this corpus, propose translation strategies for what is ostensibly 'Twitter translation'. Although they do not assess quality using engagement metrics (such as number of *retweets* and *likes*), they do address how to translate content in a medium that has character constraints, that utilizes hashtags, and that often involves implicitation and explicitation of information depending on the language pair and direction. In other words, the proposed strategies are informed by a definition of quality that is not premised upon user engagement/post performance, but rather on lexical, terminological and syntactic equivalence. Nonetheless, their work is insightful and could be helpful to any translator working with *tweets* or any other form of microblogging, especially those who are less familiar with *Twitter*. In fact, used in a complementary fashion, SMM and Hamilton and Lavallée's *Twitter* strategies might be one way to address quality from two perspectives: audience reception, in the former case, and of equivalence, in the latter case. Though some of their suggestions may have a slightly prescriptive tone, it is clear that Hamilton and Lavallée's intention is to help professional translators more effectively apply translation strategies in a new context and in relation to a new medium. The publication includes French and English content exclusively, which means that some of the proposed strategies might not apply for other language pairs. This is a welcome invitation, then, for other researchers and professionals to create similar UGC corpora comparing other language combinations.

5.6 Conclusion

This chapter has sought to address some of the connections that can be made between research conducted in TS and professional practice in the larger context of OSM. One advantage of OSM for TS researchers is that these platforms can be mobilized to disseminate TS scholarship beyond the academe. Thanks to these platforms, researchers can now discuss translation with new audiences, which has the benefit of not only creating visibility for the field but also of fostering collaboration beyond it. Of equal interest were the concepts of translator visibility, translator invisibility, translation quality and TQA methodology.

OSM provide translators with unprecedented ways of gaining professional agency: they can create their own professional profiles (e.g. *LinkedIn* profiles), self-describe their work and tasks and share as well as discuss translation strategies via their online networks. These professional profiles and these social discussions on translation give much insight as to how the translation profession and industry are evolving, particularly in light of many significant changes, be it unpaid crowdsourcing or other, newer 'threats' such automatic machine translation applications that have the potential to replace the translator in many ways (e.g. Canadian Translation Bureau with

Portage tool). Analysing professional translator profiles can give some indication as to how translators are staying competitive and relevant in the current market. Interestingly, professional networking sites, such as *LinkedIn*, can also give insight as to what employers are looking for in professional translators since these sites post job ads and offers (i.e. a corpus of translation job offers that could be further scrutinized). Observational data from Canadian job ads on *LinkedIn*, for instance, suggest that positions calling overtly for translators are not numerous, and given recent employment trends at the Canadian Translation Bureau, hiring within the public sector has been on a steady decline (Delisle 2016). However, this is not to say translation is not in demand; it is simply subsumed in other job titles and in other market sectors, which align more and more with cross-cultural communication, social media content management and social media monitoring. This gives additional weight to the argument that training must adapt to the new market realities, which includes imparting social media literacy to trainees or as part of on-going professional development.

This chapter has also considered how TQA models must be adapted to reflect new quality metrics, which include effective hashtag indexing, user engagement and overall post performance across languages and platforms. Unfortunately, effective and high-quality translated UGC often means making the translation process invisible and seemingly instant. Undoubtedly, this will impact users' and clients' expectations of translation speed. Translators who are able to self-translate and translate bidirectionally might be poised to gain significant ground in the UGC translation market, as their efficiency and versatility are key skills in a social media context.

It is clear then that as professional translation practice evolves in an OSM context, new assessment methodologies (SMM TQA), new translation strategies (hashtag translation) and new ways of 'doing business' will emerge, thus in turn creating exciting opportunities for the study of professional practice and translation more broadly.

Notes

1. 'It is also true that [TS] has in some places been colonized by language departments driven by the perceived attractiveness of academic teaching programmes centred on the practice of translation but harbouring their own academic prejudices. Ironically, this has also worsened the **artificial gap between practice and theory**.' (Munday 2012, p. 25; emphasis in original)

2. The definition of 'discourse' used here aligns the definition proposed by Candlin 1997, p. iix): discourse refers to 'language in use, as a process which is socially situated. [. . .] In this sense, discourse is a means of talking and writing about and acting upon worlds, a means which both constructs and is constructed by a set of social practices within these worlds, and in so doing both reproduces and constructs afresh particular social-discursive practices, constrained or encouraged by more macro movements in the overarching social formation.'
3. King (2010, online) says that in her experience, 'Western' profiles tend to opt for the inclusion of real photos (i.e. the person's photo) as they give an air of credibility. Though other cultures may use photos as well, this can create discomfort (*ibid.*).
4. Trends in the Canadian job market do suggest that interfacing with OSM will become inevitable, particularly for new hires across all sectors (Galt 2015). Thus, it is likely that translators will have to work with UGC at some point in their careers, whether they will want to or not. The position taken throughout the book is that in light of these trends, translators would be wise to seize the opportunities this new niche presents; however, that is not to say that other professional niches will become unviable.
5. In a thematic issue of *Linguistica Antverpiensia* (Desjardins 2011a), a series of articles broaches the topic of 'translation as social activity'. Although the term 'UGC' is not used, in some of the case studies, the authors do use excerpts from translator blogs and wikis to substantiate their research. The general position is that the digital era has given rise to even more collaboration within the field.
6. This analysis was done by doing a simple *Twitter* search using any of the conference hashtags: e.g. *#BeloHorizonte, #IATIS, #IATIS2015, #IATISBeloHorizonte.*
7. In theory, most OSM can allow users to disseminate scholarly information, regardless of their inherent specificity. For instance, although *Instagram* might not be the most effective means to disseminate a research article, a user could post a picture of something related to the research in question and provide a link to the article. A *tweet* on *Twitter* can reference an article by using a shortened URL. In other words, physical character restrictions or content type (e.g. visual and verbal) do not necessarily dictate whether or not a specific type of OSM can be effective for the dissemination of research.
8. Some OSM, for instance *Academia* (academia.edu), require the use of an institutional affiliation, which is meant to verify credentials. This is usually done through the verification of an active institutional e-mail account, but other procedures also exist.
9. This is not a commercial endorsement on behalf of the author. No compensation was received from Taylor & Francis or Routledge for the inclusion of this example.

10. This isn't to say that researchers don't attempt to gain symbolic capital otherwise; given the highly competitive academic market, some researchers are likely motivated to engage in research that is more favourably reviewed by funding bodies or academic institutions, regardless of OSM usage or SMM data. That said, SMM makes the process of knowing what is popular that much easier.
11. It should be noted at this stage of Venuti's research, the focus of his arguments pertained to the translation of literary texts into English. Extending his earlier observations to other areas in TS may result in generalization, although his later work does address visibility in other contexts as well, for instance, in terms of compensation, decision-making and so on (cf. Venuti 2013).
12. The definition of 'minority language' varies in the literature. Here, we generally follow the definition used by the UNESCO World report (UNESCO 2009) and that of the European Charter for Regional or Minority Languages (ECRML) ('European Charter for Regional or Minority Languages', 2014, online).

CHAPTER 6

Conclusion

Abstract This final chapter concludes that this book's content constitutes only the start of a conversation linking translation and social media. It suggests additional avenues and research projects that would be welcomed to further support or even counter some of the proposed claims. A summary of the three key areas explored in the previous chapters, that is theory, training and professional practice, is also provided.

Keywords Translation · Social media · Research · Theory · Training and professional practice

This book's primary intent was to begin filling a gap on the subject of online social media (OSM) in translation studies (TS). The study of OSM in relation to translation – whether as part of research on translation, of translator training and of professional practice – further pushes the interdisciplinary boundaries of TS: connections can be made with mobile and application development, social media monitoring (SMM), translator networking, hashtag indexing and so on. Given the scope of the subject, there is no doubt that this book raises more questions than it answers. Yet, asking questions is the point of departure for any research that seeks to analyse and explain phenomena, especially as they are happening. A number of proposals have been made in this volume for the development of research that seeks to connect translation and OSM, notably in the areas of

R. Desjardins, *Translation and Social Media*, Palgrave Studies in Translating and Interpreting, DOI 10.1057/978-1-137-52255-9_6

theorizing translation activity in relation to OSM; OSM and translator training; as well as the connections to be made between OSM and professional translation practice within the larger language services industry.

This book has sought to address three key areas in which OSM and translation intersect, all of which also overlap with some of the main branches of TS as mapped by Holmes (1972; 1988/2004): theory, training and professional practice. As research in the area of OSM and translation proliferates, the hope is that these three areas will be expanded upon equally. At the time of writing, much of the focus in the existing literature pertains to crowdsourcing and the implications of crowdsourcing, without much consideration for the other ways OSM are impacting TS and professional translation.

If anything, OSM have shown that TS, translator training and professional practice must all continue to adapt to technological change, especially given that OSM is a significant channel of communication across all market sectors. Professional translators have a lot to gain given their skillset, but they also have a lot to lose if they cannot compete against social media experts who also happen to be elite bilinguals. Courses or workshops that address social media literacy could be further developed to help translators and trainees acquire the skills necessary for staying competitive in the current OSM-pervasive market. This could even be done through in-house training by SMM companies, especially in the case of professional development workshops. Though not all may be favourable to the link between corporate powers and OSM, the fact remains that translation programmes are meant to respond to market requirements inter alia, especially in the case of translation programmes that purport being exclusively vocational in nature (which is notably the case for some undergraduate programmes in Canada). If trainees are not taught adequate social media literacy and related competencies, translation programmes run the risk of seeing enrolment numbers decline as bilingual students might find it more strategic to gravitate towards social media studies or communications, especially in countries that have similar bilingualism rates as Canada. Social media literacy is also a key competency that can help trainees and professional translators alike to find alternatives to existing paradigms. As Chap. 4 revealed, some millennials have been able to leverage their knowledge of social media in ways that subverted existing power structures.

In addition, without dismissing traditional peer-reviewed outlets, TS researchers can contribute to translation and translator visibility by packaging their research for dissemination on OSM platforms, which have far greater reach than most academic publications. This type of activity is largely without precedent in the field, so it will be interesting to see how events unfold in the future.

Some of the claims made in these pages are, to a degree, radical propositions that do have a number of implications – from reframing translation in light of a hypervisual and multimodal era, to adapting course curricula, to providing a parallel opportunity for peer-review – but that is precisely why these questions surrounding the relationships between OSM and translation must be scrutinized. Exploring the new avenues OSM may afford for the study of translation phenomena creates an opportunity for the field to progress in light of larger innovation and communicational shifts.

In terms of future research prospects, a particular area in which more research would be welcomed is with regard to the self-translation (cf. Grutman 2009) of user-generated content (UGC) by professional and non-professional translators (i.e. the self-translation of UGC created and published by individuals, not corporate or government entities). Do those who self-translate on OSM use embedded automatic machine translation (e.g. *Bing Translated* on *Facebook*), or are they bilingual individuals who wish to make their UGC accessible to all their *friends* or *followers*? And what about the illusion of self-translation on *Instagram*? *Instagram* can be viewed as an insidious form of advertising, masking product placement as personalized UGC (especially in the case of celebrity accounts or high-profile accounts), which in turn blurs the lines between corporate sponsorship and the anecdotal (Brown 2016). And translation plays a role in this: many pseudo-personal accounts have translated product descriptions and endorsements to ensure all *followers* can understand. The perception is that the owner of the account is the one doing the translation (and in some cases, they can be[1]), but this is not always the case, although disclosure is rarely, if ever, given. How do we classify this type of translation activity? Is it self-translation even if it is only illusory? And if indeed it is self-translation, what motivates the user to self-translate? Is the goal always capital gain? Or, in the 'like' economy, is the goal to obtain symbolic capital in the form of social media power?

More quantitative studies linking OSM and translation would also be welcomed. For instance, empirical analyses of keywords and hashtags used in professional translator profiles on professional networking sites, such as *LinkedIn,* would provide insight as to what translators view as being their dominant skills or what they view as being most relevant to include in a professional profile. Job offers, postings and ads that are published on such professional networking sites also offer empirical industry insight. What other employee titles are used to indicate jobs that require translation? How many postings link translation skills with social media skills? These analyses can be conducted using SMM tools, which indicates that knowledge of SMM tools is not only helpful in the translation of UGC (cf. Chap. 5), but also in the data collection and analysis in the context of TS research. Further, analysing this type of data could provide valuable information to help recent graduates find employment.

It is probable that the social media platforms discussed in these pages will be obsolete in 5 years' time given the meteoric rise and subsequent quasi-instant irrelevance of various social media platforms and applications (e.g. *MSN Messenger Friends* and *MySpace*). However, while some of the cited platforms and applications might indeed find an expiry date sooner rather than later, this is not to say that the questions surrounding the implications of social media for translation will lose their relevance. Visual literacy, the inclusion of semiotics in translator training, the new possibilities social media afford TS researchers – all these points are worthy of discussion in the digital era. Moreover, we have yet to see the longer-lasting impact OSM will have on future generations and what this might entail for the study of intercultural communication in the years to come.

The study of OSM is a vast subject in and of itself, and given the wide-ranging scope of TS research, it would be impossible to address all relevant issues. However, the hope is that this book has taken some steps towards addressing some of the current and key theoretical, pedagogical and professional questions that surround translation in the era of OSM. OSM were once seen as a social distraction, but now, they are an inescapable reality. It's time for #translation to join the conversation.

Note

1. *Instagram* fitness celebrity Massiel Arias rose to social media fame by connecting with her audience in both English and in Spanish. All of her posts on her main account (@massy.arias) are posted with captioning done in both English and Spanish. When the account was initially launched, the content seemed to be her own, indicating that she did her own translations (Sarumi 2014). Other celebrities, however, hire social media account managers to schedule and publish their UGC (Kaufman 2013).

References

A New Look for Instagram. (2016, May 11). From http://blog.instagram.com/post/144198429587/160511-a-new-look. Accessed 11 May 2016.

Abram, C. (2008, June 23). *Facebook in translation*. From https://www.facebook.com/notes/facebook/facebook-in-translation/20734392130/. Accessed 6 May 2016.

Ahl, D. H. (1984, November). The first decade of personal computing. *Creative Computing*, 10(11), 30.

Akamai. (2014, September 30). *Akamai releases second quarter 2014 'State of the Internet' Report*. From https://www.akamai.com/us/en/about/news/press/2014-press/akamai-releases-second-quarter-2014-state-of-the-internet-report.jsp. Accessed 6 Jan 2016.

Anastasiou, G., & Gupta, R. (2011). Comparison of crowdsourcing translation with Machine Translation. *Journal of Information Science*, 37(6), 637–659.

Angelelli, C. V. (2014). Introduction. In C. V. Angelelli (Ed.), *The sociological turn in translation and interpreting studies* (pp. 1–5). Philadelphia: John Benjamins.

Bacalu, F. (2013). The reconfiguration of translation in the digital age. *Linguistic and Philosophical Investigations*, 12, 156–161.

Baer, J., Müller, B., St-Pierre, P., & Ó Cuilleanáin, C. (2012). Translation studies forum: Translation and censorship. *Translation Studies*, 5(1), 95–110.

Baker, M. (2006). *Translation and conflict: A narrative account*. London: Routledge.

Baker, M. (2015, July). Prefigurative politics and creative subtitling. Paper presented at the fifth IATIS conference: Innovation paths in translation and intercultural studies, Belo Horizonte, Brazil.

Baldry, A., & Thibault, P. (2005). *Multimodal transcription and text analysis*. London: Equinox.

R. Desjardins, *Translation and Social Media*, Palgrave Studies in Translating and Interpreting, DOI 10.1057/978-1-137-52255-9

Bangor University – Emoji 'fastest growing new language'. (2015, May 22). *ENP Newswire.* Retrieved from https://www.bangor.ac.uk/news/university/emoji-fastest-growing-new-language-22835.

Basalamah, S. (2009). *Le droit de traduire: une politique culturelle pour la mondialisation.* Ottawa: Presses de l'Université d'Ottawa.

Basalamah, S., & Sadek, G. (2014). Copyright law and translation: Crossing epistemologies. *The Translator*, 20(3), 396–410.

Bernadini, S. (2001). Think-aloud protocols in translation research: Achievements, limits and future prospects. *Target*, 3(2), 241–263.

Bernal-Merino, M. (2015). *Translation and localisation in video games: Making entertainment software global.* London: Routledge.

Bert, E. (2000). *A practical Guide to localisation.* Amsterdam: John Benjamins.

Bert, E. (2003). Localisation and translation. In H. Somers (Ed.), *Computers and translation. A translator's guide.* Philadelphia: John Benjamins.

Bilton, N. (2014, October 29). Tinder, the fast-growing app taps an age-old truth. From http://www.nytimes.com/2014/10/30/fashion/tinder-the-fast-growing-dating-app-taps-an-age-old-truth.html?_r=2. Accessed 2 Jan 2016.

Bogucki, Ł. (2009). Amateur subtitling on the Internet. In Diaz-Cintas, J. and Anderman, G. (Eds.), *Audio-visual translation: Language transfer on screen* (pp. 49–57). Basingstoke: Palgrave Macmillan.

Bourdieu, P. (1984). *Distinction: A social critique of the judgement of taste.* Cambridge, MA: Harvard University Press.

Bourdieu, P. (1986). The forms of capital. In J. Richardson (Ed.), *Handbook of theory and research for the sociology of education* (pp. 241–258). New York: Greenwood.

boyd, D. (2009, February 26). "Social Media is Here to Stay...Now What?" Lecture Notes Microsoft Research Tech Fest: Redmond.

boyd, D., & Ellison, N. (2008). Social network sites: Definition, history and scholarship. *Journal of Computer-Mediated Communication*, 13(1), doi: 10.1111/j.1083-6101.2007.00393.x.

Brisset, A. (2010). Cultural perspectives on translation. *International Social Science Journal*, 61(199), 69–81.

Brown, K. (2016, January 19). Here is how much celebrities make in the Instagram product placement machine. From http://jezebel.com/heres-how-much-celebrities-make-in-the-instagram-produc-1740632946. Accessed 2 Apr 2016.

Brunette, L. (2000). Towards a terminology for translation quality assessment – A comparison for TQA practices. *The Translator*, 6(2), 169–182.

Buckley, S. (2012, February 23). Google adds Esperanto as its 64th machine translatable language. From http://www.engadget.com/2012/02/23/google-adds-esperanto-as-its-64th-machine-translatable-language/. Accessed 27 Apr 2016.

Bugeja, M. (2007). Distractions in the wireless classroom. *The chronicle of higher education*. From http://chronicle.com/article/Distractions-in-the-Wireless/46664. Accessed 15 Dec 2015.

Burke, J. (2016, February 25). How the media is changing terrorism. From http://www.theguardian.com/world/2016/feb/25/how-changing-media-changing-terrorism. Accessed 2 October 2016.

Buzelin, H. (2005). Unexpected allies: How Latour's network theory could complement Bourdeusian analyses in translation studies. *The Translator*, 11(2), 193–218.

Caddy, B. (n.d.). Farewell boring words, Emoji is the UK's Fastest Growing Language. From http://www.lifehacker.co.uk/2015/05/19/farewell-boring-words-emoji-is-the-uks-fastest-growing-language. Accessed 28 Apr 2016.

Canada Neck and Neck with US on Social Network, Facebook Penetration. (2014, June 12). *eMarketer*. Retrieved from http://www.emarketer.com/Article/Canada-Neck-Neck-with-US-on-Social-Network-Facebook-Penetration/1010918.

Candlin, C. N. (1997). General editor's preface. In B.-L. Gunnarsson, P. Linell and B. Nordberg (Eds.), *The construction of professional discourse*. London: Longman.

Carr, N. (2008, July/August). Is Google making us stupid? What the internet is doing to our brains. *The Atlantic*. http://www.theatlantic.com/magazine/archive/2008/07/is-google-making-us-stupid/306868/.

Carr, N. (2010). *The shallows*. London: Atlantic.

Cattrysse, P. (2001). Multimedia and translation: Methodological considerations. In Y. Gambier & H. Gottlieb (Eds.), *(Multi)media translation: Concepts, practices, and research* (pp. 1–12). Amsterdam: John Benjamins.

Chamberlain, L. (1988/2004). Gender and the metaphorics of translation. In L. Venuti (Ed.), *The translation studies reader* (pp. 306–322). London: Routledge.

Charron, M. (2005). Plus vite, encore plus vite: la traduction à l'heure de la mondialisation. *Translation Studies in the New Millennium*, 3, 15–27.

Chesterman, A., & Wagner, E. (2002). *Can theory help translators?* Routledge Manchester: St. Jerome.

Chiose, S. (2016, January 1). Ontario universities struggle to bolster entrepreneurship programs. From http://www.theglobeandmail.com/news/national/education/ontario-universities-struggle-to-design-entrepreneurship-programs/article27986407/. Accessed 2 Jan 2016.

Chung, K., Chiu, C., Xiao, X., Pei-Yu Chi, P., & Hiroshi, I. (2009). Stress OutSourced. From http://tangible.media.mit.edu/project/stress-out sourced/. Accessed 9 May 2016.

Clifford, S. (2010, March 29). For photographers, the image of a shrinking path. From http://www.nytimes.com/2010/03/30/business/media/30photogs.html. Accessed 3 Jan 2016.

Colina, S. (2008). Translation quality evaluation: Empirical evidence for a functionalist approach. *The Translator*, 14(1), 97–134.

Colina, S. (2009). Further evidence for a functionalist approach to translation quality evaluation. *Target*, 21(2), 235–264.

Colón Rodriguez, R. E. (2013, March). La traduction activiste au Canada: une communauté évolutive. Paper presented at the 16th interdisciplinary GSAED conference. From https://www.academia.edu/3530937/La_traduction_activiste_au_Canada_une_communaut%C3%A9_%C3%A9volutive. Accessed 3 Jan 2016.

Costales, A. F. (2011). Crowdsourcing and collaborative translation: Mass phenomena of silent threat to translation studies? *Hermeneus*, 15, 85–110.

Cronin, M. (2003). Translation and globalization. London: Routledge.

Cronin, M. (2013). *Translation in the digital age*. London: Routledge.

Davenport, T. H., & Kirby, J. (2015). Beyond automation: Strategies for remaining gainfully employed in an era of very smart machines. *Harvard Business Review*, 93(6), 59–65.

Davis, M. (2015, May 22). Unicode 9.0 Candidate Emoji. From http://blog.unicode.org/2015/05/unicode-90-candidate-emoji.html. Accessed 28 Apr 2016.

Debray, R. (2001). *Introduction à la médiologie*. Paris: Presses Universitaires de France.

Delisle, J. (Ed.), (1999). *Portraits de traducteurs*. Ottawa: University of Ottawa Press.

Delisle, J. (2002). *Portraits de traductrices*. Ottawa: University of Ottawa Press.

Delisle, J. (2016, April 26). La traduction à Ottawa: de l'anarchie à la chienlit. From http://www.ledevoir.com/politique/canada/469105/la-traduction-a-ottawa-de-l-anarchie-a-la-chienlit. Accessed 2 May 2016.

Delisle, J. and Fiola, M. (2013). *La traduction raisonnée* (3rd edn.). Ottawa: Les presses de l'Université d'Ottawa.

Desjardins, R. (2008). Inter-semiotic translation within the space of the multimodal text. In TransCulTural, *War and peace: Translation as conflict, resistance, and resolution* (Vol. 1(1), 48–58.

Desjardins, R. (2010, March). Facebook Me!: Arguing in favour of social networking websites as pedagogical translation tools. Paper presented at 9th Edition of Voyages in Translation Studies, Concordia University, Montreal.

Desjardins, R. (2011a). Facebook Me!: Initial insights in favour of using social media as a tool for translator training. *Linguistica Antverpiensia*, *10*, 175–193.

Desjardins, R. (2011b, April). How Facebook can revamp translator training. Paper presented at Forum 2011: Innovations in translator, interpreter and localizer education, Monterey Institute of International Studies, Monterey.

Desjardins, R. (2013a). Social media and translation. In Y. Gambier and L. van Doorslaer (Eds.), *The handbook of translation studies* (pp. 156–159). Amsterdam: John Benjamins.

Desjardins, R. (2013b). *Translation and the Bouchard-Taylor Commission: translating images, translating cultures, translating Québec. (Unpublished doctoral dissertation), University of Ottawa, Ottawa.

Deutsch, B. (2014, December). *For success in social media, conversation is not enough-you need narrative.* From http://www.fastcocreate.com/3039565/for-success-in-social-media-conversation-is-not-enough-you-need-narrative. Accessed 12 Apr 2016.

Dillet, R. (2013, 29 October). SoundCloud now reaches 250 Million visitors in its quest to become the audio platform of the web. From http://techcrunch.com/2013/10/29/soundcloud-now-reaches-250-million-listeners-in-its-quest-to-become-the-audio-platform-of-the-web/. Accessed 20 Apr 2016.

Do Social Media Change Our Behaviors? (2015, May 27). WeRSM. From http://wersm.com/do-social-media-change-our-behaviors/. Accessed 22 Dec 2015.

Doble, A. (2015, May 19). UK's fastest growing language is Emoji. From http://www.bbc.co.uk/newsbeat/article/32793732/uks-fastest-growing-language-is-emoji. Accessed 2 May 2016.

Dolmaya, J. M (2011). The ethics of crowdsourcing. *Linguistica Antverpiensia*, 10, 97–111.

Dresner, E., & Herring, S. C. (2010). Functions of the nonverbal in CMC: Emoticons and illocutionary force. *Communication Theory*, 20, 249–268.

Drugan, J. (2013). *Quality in professional translation: Assessment and improvement.* London: Bloomsbury.

Duarte, J. F., Seruya, T., & Assis Rosa, A. (2006). *Translation studies at the interface of disciplines.* Benjamins Translation Library, 68 Amsterdam: John Benjamins.

Dunne, K. J. (2015). Localization. In C. Sin-Wai (Ed.), *The Routledge encyclopedia of translation technology* (pp. 550–562). London: Routledge.

DuoLingo. (2015). *Learn Esperanto in just 5 minutes a day.* From https://en.duolingo.com/course/eo/en/Learn-Esperanto-Online. Accessed 10 January 2016.

Eid, M., & Al Osman, H. (2016). Affective haptics: Current research and future directions. *IEEE Access*, 4, 26–40.

Elkins, J. Ed. (2008). *Visual literacy.* New York: Routledge.

European Charter for Regional or Minority Languages. (2014). From http://www.coe.int/t/dg4/education/minlang/aboutcharter/default_en.asp. Accessed 13 April 2016.

Facebook (2016). Translate Facebook App. Retrieved May 6, 2016, from https://www.facebook.com/help/100117036792266

Federici, F. M. (Ed.) (2016). *Mediating emergencies and conflicts: Frontline translating and interpreting.* Basingstoke: Palgrave Macmillan.

Fernandes, J. (2011 October 6). Facebook Quietly Rolls Out the "Translate" Button. From http://techie-buzz.com/social-networking/facebook-rolls-out-translate-button.html. Accessed 10 Jan 2016.

Fettes, M. (2005). Artificial languages. In Philipp Skutch (Ed.), *Routledge encyclopedia of linguistics* (Vol. 1). New York: Routledge.

Financial Times. (2016). Social media monitoring. From http://lexicon.ft.com/Term?term=social-media-monitoring. Accessed 3 May 2016.

Folaron, D. (2010a). Web and translation. In Y. Gambier and L. van Doorslaer (Eds.), *The handbook of translation studies* (pp. 446–450). Amsterdam: John Benjamins.

Folaron, D. (2010b). Networking and volunteer translators. In Y. Gambier and L. van Doorslaer (Eds.), *Handbook of translation studies* (pp. 231–234). Amsterdam: John Benjamins.

Folaron, D. (2012). Digitalizing translation. In *Translation Spaces* (Vol. 1., pp. 5–31). Amsterdam: John Benjamins.

Fraenkel, C. and Etinson, A. (2012, May 29). One hundred days of student protests in Québec: Printemps Érable or much ado about nothing. From https://www.dissentmagazine.org/online_articles/one-hundred-days-of-student-protests-in-quebec-printemps-erable-or-much-ado-about-nothing. Accessed 27 Dec 2015.

Fraisse, E. (2013, June 26). La traduction, indicateur des relations culturelles mondiales: de l'inégalité parmi les langues. From http://www.fabula.org/colloques/document1997.php. Accessed 3 Jan 2016.

Fuchs, C. (2014). *Social media: A critical introduction.* London: Sage.

Fuchs, C. (2015). *Culture and economy in the age of social media.* London: Routledge.

Galt, V. (2015, June 26) Some bright spots in a cloudy jobs picture. From http://www.theglobeandmail.com/report-on-business/careers/career-advice/life-at-work/some-bright-spots-in-a-cloudy-jobs-picture/article25143713/. Accessed 3 Jan 2016.

Gambier, Y. (2006). Multimodality and audiovisual translation. *MuTra 2006.* Retrieved from http://www.euroconferences.info/proceedings/2006_Proceedings/2006_Gambier_Yvs.pdf

Gambier, Y. (2014). De quelques effets de l'internationalisation et la technologisation. *Target*, 26(2), 259–268.

García, I. (2010). The proper place of professionals (and non-professionals and machines) in web translation. *Révista tradumàtica*, 8, (n.p.).

García, I. (2015). Cloud marketplaces: Procurement of translators in the age of social media. *JoSTrans. The Journal of Specialised Translation*, 23, 18–38.

Giroux, H. A. (2007). *The University in chains: Confronting the military-industrial-academic complex.* Boulder: Paradigm Publishers.

Göpferich, S. (2010). Transfer and transfer studies. In Y. Gambier, & L. van Doorslaer (Eds.), *Handbook of translation studies vol. 1* (pp. 374–377). Amsterdam: John Benjamins.

Gouadec, D. (2007). *Translation as a profession.* Philadelphia: John Benjamins.

Gouanvic, J.-M. (2005). A Bourdieusian theory of translation, or the coincidence of practical instance: Field, 'Habitus', Capital and 'Illusio'. (Jessica Moore, Trans.) *The Translator*, 11(2), 147–166.

Grindley, L. (2014, July 30). Tyler Oakley could be the first Gay person you ever meet. From http://www.advocate.com/40-under-40-emerging-voices/2014/07/30/40-under-40-tyler-oakley-could-be-first-gay-person-you-ever. Accessed 3 May 2016.

Grossman, L. (2006, December 25). You – Yes, You – are TIME's person of the year. Retrieved from http://content.time.com/time/specials/packages/0,28757,2019341,00.html.

Grucza, S., Płużyczka, M., & Zając, J. (2013). Eye-tracking supported translation studies at the University of Warsaw. From http://www.beck-shop.de/fachbuch/vorwort/9783631634486_Intro_005.pdf. Accessed 4 Jan 2016.

Grutman, R. (2009). Self-translation. In M. Baker and G. Saldanha (Eds.), *Routledge Encyclopedia of Translation Studies* (2nd edn., pp. 257–260). London: Routledge.

Hamilton, G., & Lavallée, F. (2012). *Tweets et gazouillis pour des traductions qui chantent.* Montréal: Linguatech éditeur.

Hanifan, L. J. (1920). *The community center.* Boston: *Silver* Burdett & Company.

Heilbron, J., & Sapiro, G. (2007). Outline for a sociology of translation: Current issues and future prospects. In Wolf, M. and Fukari, A. (Eds.), *Constructing a sociology of translation* (pp. 93–107). Amsterdam: John Benjamins.

Hermans, T. (Ed.) (1985). *The Manipulation of Literature: Studies in Literary Translation.* Beckenham: Croom Helm.

Holmes, J. (1972, August 21–26). The name and nature of translation studies. In J. Qvistgaard et al. (Eds.), *Third international congress of applied linguistics.* Copenhagen: Congress Abstracts.

Holmes, J. (1988/2004). The name and nature of translation studies. In L. Venuti (Ed.), *The translation studies reader* (2nd ed., pp. 180–204). London: Routledge.

Houpt, S. (2012, September 10). What the printemps érable really means. From http://www.theglobeandmail.com/arts/what-the-printemps-erable-really-means/article4224937/. Accessed 10 May 2016.

Howe, J. (2006, June). The rise of crowdsourcing. *Wired Magazine.* https://www.wired.com/2006/06/crowds/. Accessed 29 September 2016.

Howe, J. (2008). *Crowdsourcing: Why the power of the crowd is driving the future of business.* New York: Three Rivers Press.

Is Social Media Turning Us into Psychopaths? (n.d.) From http://www.whoishostingthis.com/blog/2013/06/03/social-media-psychopaths/. Accessed 3 January 2016.

Is Translation Theory Useful to the Practising Translator: Your Opinions Please (2011, January 10). From http://www.proz.com/forum/translation_theory_and_practice/189199-is_translation_theory_useful_to_the_practising_translator_your_opinions_please.html. Accessed 2 May 2016.

Jakobson, R. (1959/2004). On linguistic aspects of translation. In L. Venuti (Ed.), *The translation studies reader* (2nd edn., pp. 138–143). London: Routledge.

Jaschik, S. (2007, August 7). 'The University in Chains'. Retrieved from https://www.insidehighered.com/news/2007/08/07/giroux

Jenkins, H. (2006). *Fans, bloggers, and gamers.* New York: New York University Press.

Jenkins, H. (2008). *Convergence culture.* New York: New York University Press.

Jiménez-Crespo, M. (2013). *Translation and web localization.* London: Routledge.

Jiménez-Crespo, M. (2015). Translation quality, Use and dissemination in an internet Era: Using single-translation and multi-translation parallel corpora to research translation quality on the web. *The Journal of Specialised Translation*, 23, 39–63.

Jones, J. (2015, May 27). Emoji is dragging us back to the dark ages – And all we can do is smile. From http://www.theguardian.com/artanddesign/jonathanjonesblog/2015/may/27/emojilanguage-dragging-us-back-to-the-dark-ages-yellow-smiley-face. Accessed 3 May 2016.

Kaplan, A.M. & Haenlein, M. (2010). Users of the world, unite! The challenges and opportunities of social media. *Business Horizons*, 53(1), 59–68.

Kaufman, A. (2013, November 15). For Hollywood's Social Media Managers, Tweeting is a living. From http://www.huffingtonpost.com/ahrif-sarumi/post_7423_b_5204947.html. Accessed 1 May 2016.

Kelly, D. (2005). *A handbook for translator trainers: A guide to reflective practice.* Manchester: St Jerome.

Kelly, N. (2009, June 19). Freelance translators clash with LinkedIn over crowdsourced translation. *Translation and Localization.* From http://www.commonsenseadvisory.com/Default.aspx?Contenttype=ArticleDetA&tabI=63&Aid=591&moduleId=390. Accessed 3 Jan 2016.

Kelm, O. R. (2011). Social media: It's what students do. *Business Communication Quarterly*, *74*(4), 505–520. doi: 10.1177/1080569911423960.

King, C. (2010, April 29). Do you need social media localization? From http://customerthink.com/do_you_need_social_media_localization/. Accessed 2 Jan 2016.

Kiraly, D. (2000). *A social constructivist approach to translator education. Empowerment from theory to practice.* Manchester: St. Jerome.

Kiraly, D. C. (1995). *Pathways to translation: Pedagogy and process.* Kent: Kent State University Press.

Koglin, A. (2015, July). Cognitive effort in human translation and post-editing: An analysis of pupil dilation and fixation duration on metaphors. Paper presented at 5th IATIS Conference: Innovation Paths in Translation and Intercultural Studies, Belo Horizonte.

Kress, G., & van Leeuwen, T. (2001). *Multimodal discourse: The modes and media of contemporary communication*. London: Arnold.

Kress, G., & van Leeuwen, T. (2006). *Reading images: The grammar of visual design* (2nd edn.). New York: Routledge.

Kuhiwczak, P. (2011). Translation and censorship. *Translation Studies*, *4*(3), 358–373.

Kussman, P., & Tirkonnen-Condit, S. (1995). Think-aloud protocol analysis in translation studies. *TTR: Traduction, Terminologie, Rédaction*, 8(1), 177–199.

Lambert, J. (1997/2006). Problems and challenges of translation in an age of new media and competing models. In Delabastita, D., D'hulst, L., and Meylaerts, R. (Eds.), *Functional approaches to culture and translation: Selected papers by José Lambert*. Amsterdam: John Benjamins.

Lambert, J. (2012). Interdisciplinarity in translation studies. In Y. Gambier and L. Van Doorslaer (Eds.), *The handbook of translation studies* (pp. 81–88). doi:10.1075/hts.3.int4.

Law, M. A. (2015, July). *How editors read: An eye-tracking study of the effects of editorial experience and task instruction on reading behaviour*. Paper presented at the 5th IATIS Conference: Innovation Paths in Translation and Intecultural Studies, Belo Horizonte.

Lefevere, A. (1982/2004). Mother courage's cucumbers. Text, system and refraction in a theory of literature. In L. Venuti (Ed.), *The translation studies reader* (2nd ed., pp. 239–255). London: Routledge.

Lefevere, A. (1993). Discourses on translation: Recent, less recent and to come. *Target*, 5(2), 229–241. doi:10.1075/target.5.2.08lef.

Lessig, L. (2004). *Free culture: The nature and future of creativity*. New York: Penguin Books.

Littau, K. (2011). First steps toward a media history of translation. *Translation Studies*, 4(3), 261–281. doi: 10.1080/14781700.2011.589651.

Littau, K. (2015). Translation and the materialities of communication. *Translation Studies*, 9(1), 82–96.

Long, J. (2012). Changes of translation definition and turns of translation studies. *Cross-Cultural Communication*, 8(5), 35–43. http://dx.doi.org/10.3968/j.ccc.1923670020120805.2156.

Mateo, R. M. (2014). A deeper look into metrics for translation quality assessment (TQA): Case study. *Miscelánea: A journal of English and American Studies*, *49*, 73–94.

McDonough, J. (2007). How do language professionals organize themselves? An overview of translation networks. *Meta: Journal des traducteurs/Meta: Translators' Journal*, 52(4), 793–815.

McHugh, M. (2016, February 14). It's hard out there for a new Emoji. From http://www.wired.com/2016/02/new-emoji-popularity-rankings/. Accessed 25 April 2016.

McLuhan, M. (1964). *Understanding the media: Extensions of man*. New York: McGraw-Hill.

Meme (2016). Merriam-Webster Dictionary. From http://www.merriamwebster.com/dictionary/meme. Accessed September 30, 2016.

Mills, C. W. (1956/2000). *The power Elite*. Oxford: Oxford University Press.

Morozov, E. (2009, May). The brave new world of slacktivism. From http://www.npr.org/templates/story/story.php?storyId=104302141. Accessed 20 Dec 2015.

Morozov, E. (2010). *The Net delusion: How not to liberate the world*. London: Allen Lane.

Morozov, E. (2013). *To save everything, click here: Technology, solutionism and the urge to fix problems that don't exist*. London: Allen Lane.

Morris, K. (2013, April 29). The great Facebook exodus has begun. From http://www.dailydot.com/business/facebook-exodus-losing-users-study-data/. Accessed 12 April 2016.

Moscaritolo, A. (2012, December 21). Instagram adds news 'Mayfair' filter, support for 25 languages. From http://www.pcmag.com/article2/0,2817,2413502,00.asp. Accessed 5 May 2016.

Munday, J. (2004). Advertising: some challenges to translation theory. *Special Issue. Key Debates in the Translation of Advertising Material, The Translator*, 10(2), 199–219.

Munday, J. (2012). *Introducing translation studies: Theories and applications* (3rd edn.). London: Routledge.

Munday, J. (2016). *Introducing translation studies: Theories and applications* (4th ed.). London: Routledge.

Nielsen, J. (2006). F-Shaped pattern for reading web content. From https://www.nngroup.com/articles/f-shaped-patternreading-web-content/. Accessed 30 September 2016.

Nielsen, J. (2008). How little do users read? From https://www.nngroup.com/articles/how-little-do-users-read/. Accessed 9 May 2016.

Nord, Christiane. (1997). *Translating as a purposeful activity: Functionalist approaches explained*. Manchester: St. Jerome.

O'Brien, S. (2011). Collaborative translation. In Y. Gambier and L. van Doorslaer (Eds.), *The handbook of translation studies* (pp. 17–20). Amsterdam: John Benjamins.

O'Brien, S. (2016). Training translators for crisis communication: Translators without borders as an example. In F. M. Federici (Ed.), *Mediating emergencies and conflicts: Frontline translation and interpreting* (pp. 85–111). doi:10.1057/978-1-137-55351-5_4.

O'Hagan, M. (2008). Fan translation networks: An accidental translator training environment? In J. Kearns (Ed.), *Translator and interpreter training: Issues, methods and debates* (pp. 158–183). London: Continuum.

O'Hagan, M. (2009). Evolution of user-generated translation: Fansubs, translation hacking and crowdsourcing. *The Journal of Internationalization and Localization*, 1, 94–121. doi: 10.1075/jial.1.04hag.

O'Hagan, M. (2011). Community translation: Translation as a social activity and its possible consequences in the advent of Web 2.0 and beyond. *Linguistica Antverpiensia*, New Series – Themes in Translation Studies.

O'Hagan, M., & Mangiron, C. (2013). *Game localization: Translating for the digital entertainment industry*. Amsterdam: John Benjamins.

Online translator helps federal workers 'do their job,' say defenders. (2016, Feb. 4). From http://www.cbc.ca/news/canada/ottawa/online-translator-defended-1.3433919. Accessed 2 May 2016.

Oittinen, R., & Kaindl, K. (2008). Introduction: The verbal/the visual/the translator. *META*, 53(1), 5.

Ostler, N. (2010). *The Last Lingua Franca: English until the return of Babel*. New York: Walker and Company.

Oswald, L. (2012). *Marketing semiotics: Signs, strategies, and brand value*. Oxford: Oxford University Press.

Panzarino, M. (2012). Instagram updated to add 'double-tap' likes and improved comments. From http://thenextweb.com/apps/2011/05/26/instagram-updates-to-add-double-tap-likes-and-improved-comments/#gref. Accessed 30 Mar 2016.

Perrino, S. (2009). User-generated translation: The future of translation in a Web 2.0 environment. *JoSTrans. The Journal of Specialised Translation*, 12, 55–78.

Posner, N. (2009, June). Translating LinkedIn into many languages. From https://blog.linkedin.com/2009/06/19/nico-posner-translating-linkedin-into-many-languages. Accessed September 30, 2016.

Prensky, M. (2001). Digital natives, digital immigrants, Part II: Do they really think differently? *On the Horizon*, 9(6), NCB University Press 1–9.

Prensky, M. (2006). Listen to the natives. *Educational Leadership*, 63(4), 8–13.

Prensky, M. (2007). How to teach with technology. *BECTA's Emerging Technologies for Learning*, *2*, 40–46.

Pym, A. (2011a). What technology does to translating. *Translation and Interpreting*, 3(1), 1–9.

Pym, A. (2011b). Web Localization. In K. Malmkjaer and K. Windle (Eds.), *The Oxford handbook of translation studies*. Oxford: Oxford University Press. 10.1093/oxfordhb/9780199239306.013.0028.

Reeves, N. (2002). Translation, international English, and the planet of babel. *English Today*, 18(4), 21–28.

Roblyer, M. D., McDaniel, M., Webb, M., Herman, J., & Witty, J. V. (2010). Findings on Facebook in Higher Education: A comparison of college faculty and student uses and perceptions of social networking sites. *Internet and Higher Education*, 13(3), 134–140.

Rogers, M. (2015). *Specialised translation: Shedding the 'Non-Literary' Tag*. Hampshire: Palgrave Macmillan.
Rose, G. (2007). *Visual methodologies: An introduction to the interpretation of visual materials*. Thousand Oaks: Sage.
Rose, G. (2012). Visual methodologies. From http://www.sagepub.com/rose/default.htm. Accessed 30 Mar 2016.
Sapiro, G., and Heilbron, J. (2008). La Traduction comme vecteur des échanges culturels internationaux InTranslatio. Le marché de la traduction en France à l'heure de la mondialisation. Paris: CNRS Éditions.
Sarumi, A. (2014, April 28/June 28). After Instagram Fame, Massiel 'MankoFit' Arias is Misbehaving Her Way into Mainstream Success. From http://www.huffingtonpost.com/ahrif-sarumi/post_7423_b_5204947.html. Accessed 2 May 2016.
Schäler, R. (2010). Localization and translation. In Y. Gambier and L. van Doorslaer (Eds.), *The handbook of translation studies* (pp. 210–214). Amsterdam: John Benjamins.
Schonfeld, E. (2009, September 29). *Facebook spreads its crowdsourced translations across the Web, and the world*. From http://techcrunch.com/2009/09/29/facebook-spreads-its-crowdsourced-translations-across-the-web-and-the-world/. Accessed 30 March 2016.
Selwyn, N. (2011). *Schools and schooling in the digital age: A critical analysis*. London: Routledge.
Service Canada. (2015, October 30). University Professors. From http://www.servicecanada.gc.ca/eng/qc/job_futures/statistics/4121.shtml. Accessed 9 May 2016.
Shin, L. (2014, December 5). 4 in 5 millennials optimistic for future, but half live Paycheck to Paycheck. From http://www.forbes.com/sites/laurashin/2014/12/05/4-in-5-millennials-optimistic-for-future-but-half-live-paycheck-to-paycheck/#6697b07b5cd5. Accessed 9 Jan 2016.
Simon, S. (2006). *Translating montreal: Episodes in the life of the divided city*. McGill-Queen's University Press.
Simeoni, D. (2007) Translation and society: The emergence of a conceptual relationship. In St-Pierre, P. and P.C. Kar (Eds.), In *Translation – reflections, refractions, transformations* (pp. 13–26). Philadelphia: John Benjamins.
Singh, N., Lehnert, K., Bostick, K. (2012). Global social media usage: Insights into reaching consumers worldwide. *Thunderbird International Business Review*, *54*(5), 683–700. 10.1002/tie.
Sin-Wai, C. (Ed). (2015). *The Routledge Encyclopedia of translation technology*. London: Routledge.
Snell-Hornby, M. (1988). *Translation studies: An integrated approach*. Amsterdam: John Benjamins.
Snell-Hornby, M. (2006). *The turns of translation studies. New paradigms or shifting viewpoints?* Amsterdam: Benjamins.

Snell-Hornby, M. (2009). What's in a turn? On fits, starts, and writings in recent translation studies. *Translation Studies*, 2(1), 41–51.

Snell-Hornby, M. (2012). From the fall of the wall to Facebook: Translation studies in Europe twenty years later. *Perspectives: Studies in Translatology*, 20(3), 365–373. 10.1080/0907676X.2012.702403.

Snell-Hornby, M., Pöchhacker, F. and Kaindl, K. Eds. (1994). *Translation Studies: An Interdiscipline*. Benjamins Translation Library, *2* Amsterdam: John Benjamins.

Social Network Audience Growth Plateaus in Canada. (2015, January 22). *eMarketer*. Retrieved from http://www.emarketer.com/Article/Social-Network-Audience-Growth-Plateaus-Canada/1011898.

Standage, T. (2013). *Writing on the Wall: Social media – The first two thousand years*. New York: Bloomsbury.

Statista. (2016, April 20). *Leading social networks as of April 2016*. From http://www.statista.com/statistics/272014/global-social-networks-ranked-by-number-of-users/. Accessed 20 Apr 2016.

Stewart, C. M., Schifter C. C., & Markaridian Selverian, M. Eds. (2010). *Teaching and learning with technology: Beyond constructivism*. London: Routledge.

Sumner, C., Byers, A., Boochever, R., and Park, G. J. (2012). Predicting dark triad personality traits from Twitter usage and a linguistic analysis of tweets. *Machine Learning and Applications (ICMLA)*, *2*(386–393). 10.1109/ICMLA.2012.218.

Sutherlin, G. (2013). A voice in the crowd: Broader implications for crowdsourcing translation during crisis. *Journal of Information Science*, 39(3), 397–409. 10.1177/0165551512471593.

Szczyrbak, M. (2011). Where the Ivory Tower meet the wordface: In search of meaning and alternatives to silence in specialist translator training. *SKASE Journal of Translation and Interpretation*, 5(1), 79–93.

Taylor, C. J. (2013). Multimodality and audiovisual translation. In Y. Gambier and L. van Doorslaer (Eds.), *The handbook of translation studies* (pp. 98–104). Amsterdam: John Benjamins.

Technopedia. (2016a). Meme. From https://www.techopedia.com/definition/16944/internet-meme. Accessed 6 Jan 2016.

Technopedia. (2016b). Mobile Device. From https://www.techopedia.com/definition/23586/mobile-device. Accessed 3 May 2016.

Technopedia. (2016c). Social media monitoring. From https://www.techopedia.com/definition/29592/social-media-monitoring. Accessed 6 Jan 2016.

Technopedia. (2016d). Search engine optimization. From https://www.techopedia.com/definition/5391/search-engine-optimization-seo. Accessed 10 May 2016.

Terranova, T. (2004). *Network culture*. London: Pluto.

Tesseras, L. (2015, July 21). Are emojis becoming marketers' go-to global language? From http://www.marketingweek.com/2015/07/21/are-emojis-becoming-marketers-go-to-global-language/. Accessed 27 Apr 2016.

Thobani, S. (2007). *Exalted subjects: Studies in the making of race and nation in Canada*. Toronto: University of Toronto Press.

Toffler, A. (1980). *The third wave: The classic study of tomorrow*. New York: Bantam.

Torresi, I. (2008). Advertising: A case for intersemiotic translation. *META*, 53(1), 62–75.

Toury, G. (1978). The nature and role of norms in literary translation. In Holmes, J. S, Lambert, J. and van den Broeck, R. (Eds.), *Literature and translation: New perspectives in literary studies*. Leuven: Acco.

Toury, G. (1980). *In search of a theory of translation*. Tel Aviv: Tel Aviv University, The Porter Institute for Poetics and Semiotics.

Toury, G. (1995). *Descriptive translation studies and beyond*. Amsterdam: John Benjamins.

Translating the *printemps érable*. (2012). From http://translatingtheprintempserable.tumblr.com/. Accessed 2 Jan 2016.

Translators against crowdsourcing by commercial business. (2015). From https://www.linkedin.com/groups/2032092/profile. Accessed 9 May 2016.

Tymoczko, M. (2006). Reconceptualizing translation theory: Integrating non-western thought about translation. In Hermans, T. (Ed.), *Translating Others* (Vol. 1, pp. 13–32). Manchester: St-Jerome.

Tymoczko, M. (2007). *Enlarging translation, empowering translators*. Manchester: St-Jerome Publishing.

Tymoczko, M. (Ed.) (2010). *Translation, resistance, activism*. Massachusetts: UMass Press.

Tymoczko, M. (2014). The neuroscience of translation. *Target*, 24(1), 83–102.

Tyulenev, S. (2011). *Applying Luhmann to translation studies*. New York: Routledge.

Tyulenev, S. (2014). *Translation and society: An introduction*. New York: Routledge.

UM Social Media Tracker-Wave 4. (2009). Power to the People, Wave 4. From http://wave.umww.com/assets/pdf/wave_4-power_to_the_people.pdf. Accessed 10 Dec 2015.

UM Social Media Tracker-Wave 5. (2010). The socialization of brands. From http://fr.slideshare.net/fred.zimny/uu-report-wave-5-the-socialisation-of-brandsreport. Accessed 10 Dec 2015.

UNESCO. (2009). UNESCO world report: Investing in cultural diversity and intercultural dialogue. http://unesdoc.unesco.org/images/0018/001847/184755e.pdf. Accessed 29 September 2016.

Van Dijck, J., Nieborg, D. (2009). Wikinomics and its discontents: A critical analysis of web 2.0 business manifestors. *New Media & Society*, 11(5), 855–874.

Van Grove, J. (2013). Why teens are tiring of Facebook. From http://www.cnet.com/news/why-teens-are-tiring-of-facebook/. Accessed 3 Jan 2016.

Vandendorpe, C. (1999). *Du papyrus à l'hypertexte. Essai sur les mutations du texte et de la lecture*. Montréal: Boréal.

Vandendorpe, C. (1999/2009). *From papyrus to hypertext: Toward the Universal digital library*. (P.A. Aronoff and H. Scott, Trans.) Chicago: University of Illinois Press.
Venuti, L. (1995). *The Translator's Invisibility*. New York: Routledge.
Venuti, L. (1998). *The scandals of translation: Towards an ethics of difference*. London: Routledge.
Venuti, L. (2008). *The translator's invisibility: A history of translation* (2nd edn.). New York: Routledge.
Venuti, L. (2013). *Translation changes everything*. New York: Routledge.
Vogel, P. (2015). *Generation jobless: Turning the youth employment crisis into opportunity*. New York: Palgrave Macmillan.
Watts, G. (2014, November 18). In other words: Inside the lives and minds of real-time translators. From http://mosaicscience.com/story/other-words-inside-lives-and-minds-real-time-translators. Accessed 12 Dec 2015.
Weller, M. (2007). *Virtual learning environments: Using, choosing and developing your VLE*. London: Routledge.
What is Fair Use? (2016). From https://www.youtube.com/yt/copyright/fair-use.html. Accessed 1 May 2016.
What's trending in Translation Studies. (2015, March 9). From http://explore.tandfonline.com/page/ah/translation-trending. Accessed 17 April 2016.
Wihbey, J. P. (2014). The challenges of democratizing news and information: Examining data on social media, viral patterns and digital influence. Shorenstein Center on Media, Politics and Public Policy Discussion Paper Series, #D-85 (June 2014). http://nrs.harvard.edu/urn-3:HUL.InstRepos:12872220.
Williams, M. (2004). *Translation quality assessment: An argumentation-centred approach*. Ottawa: University of Ottawa Press.
Wolf, M. and Fukari, A. Eds. (2007). *Constructing a sociology of translation*. Amsterdam: John Benjamins.
Young, R. J. C. (2003). *Postcolonialism: A Very Short Introduction*. Oxford: Oxford University Press.
Zappavigna, M. (2012). *The discourse of Twitter and Social Media*. New York: Continuum.

Index

R. Desjardins, *Translation and Social Media*, Palgrave Studies in Translating and Interpreting, DOI 10.1057/978-1-137-52255-9

Lightning Source UK Ltd.
Milton Keynes UK
UKOW06n1136111217
314159UK00016B/762/P